Diary of a Passionate Poet

Beauty, Love and Hope in an Ordinary Life

KATARINA B. VIKTOR

With Forewords by Nathan Barnes and Elizabeth Need

BALBOA.PRESS

A DIVISION OF HAY HOUSE

Balboa Press books may be ordered through booksellers or by contacting:

Balboa Press
A Division of Hay House
1663 Liberty Drive
Bloomington, IN 47403
www.balboapress.com.au
AU TFN: 1 800 844 925 (Toll Free inside Australia)
AU Local: (02) 8310 7086 (+61 2 8310 7086 from outside Australia)

Scripture taken from the King James Version of the Bible.

Nathan Barnes and Elizabeth Need, who wrote the Forewords,
gave permission for their names to be mentioned.

Print information available on the last page.

ISBN: 978-1-5043-1546-3 (sc)
ISBN: 978-1-5043-1547-0 (e)

Balboa Press rev. date: 03/29/2022

In beloved memory of loved ones departed, and to those
who are living, whom I keep in my heart, always.
To my husband, children and grandchildren.

"Greater love hath no man than this, that a man lay
down his life for his friends." **John 15:13**

The Holy Bible: King James Version

"Finally, brethren, whatsoever things are true, whatsoever things are honest, whatsoever things are just, whatsoever things are pure, whatsoever things are lovely, whatsoever things are of good report; if there be any virtue, and if there be any praise, think on these things.

Those things, which ye have both learned, and received, and heard, and seen in me, do: and the God of peace shall be with you." **Philippians 4: 8–9**

The Holy Bible: King James Version

Contents

List of Illustrations

Illustrations © 2018 Katarina B. Viktor
Photographed by Stuart Innes

Foreword

By Nathan Barnes, Pastor

I sat in the lounge room of a small terraced house in the city. A few days earlier the occupant had called me at the church and now a friend and I had come to meet her. She was a woman who has seen much pain in her life, and who still faced many struggles and carried deep heartache. She shared some of these with us through tears.

Conflicts, disappointments, grief—Katarina had seen more than her fair share. She seemed almost overwhelmed by it all. And yet she was not bitter. As she shared with us she talked about more than just her difficulties. There was something deeper that held her fast through all of these things; something which gave her hope and confidence. Katarina had found security and love and joy and hope in Christ.

Katarina's poetry flows from these realities. She sees life as it is with its glorious joys but also its deep pain. She is not afraid to take the time to stop and notice the things that others walk past and to see the world from different angles. And in all of this she sees the faithful hand of God and is drawn to put her hope in him.

These poems were not originally written to be shared, but in publishing them now Katarina invites us to see the world through her eyes. As you read these pages you are invited to look at life rather than hurrying through it, and to find the true meaning of life in the one who made it.

Foreword

By Elizabeth Need

Katarina and I met under fairly innocuous circumstances. She was walking her son's dog, Mika, and I was attending a roadside auction. New to the city, we struck up a friendship and Katarina and I would often walk the dog, while chatting about life at large. I quickly came to understand Katarina was a multi-talented soul struggling and conquering her own challenges in life.

These poems touch and warm my soul. Sometimes we just need a gentle nudge to remind us that we do not need to seek some grander meaning of life. If we just stopped, observed and appreciated the world around us, we might just find what we are looking for.

This collection of poems illustrates all the ugliness and beauty of life in equal measure—a calming relief in a very pre-occupied world.

Preface

My grandfather on my father's side was Swiss German. It was never acceptable to cry in my grandfather's presence. My father learned to hold his emotions and passed this on to me. A professor at the university, though my father's father was emotionally strict, he had a good heart.

My mother's parents were from Russia and belonged to the Russian Orthodox Church. They raised me until I was six years old. They loved me greatly and were very affectionate.

Though my father was distant in his demeanor, circumstances were beyond his control. When I arrived in Australia from Germany, we were reunited after a period of separation. Joy flowed out of him at seeing me.

Quietly at night, he would ask me to repeat The Lord's Prayer. Nothing could take away his determination to teach me this. He encouraged us to never go to sleep before reciting this prayer. One night I asked him, "Papa, is God real?" He replied, "Yes he is!" So when my father said "Yes, dear child, God is real," this confirmed what I already knew. I felt at peace and strengthened.

My mother would interrupt us at prayer time. She told me that God is a fairytale and it was rubbish to believe in God. I was forbidden to mention his name.

Patience etched my father's being when provoked by my mother. Even when tired he had an air of peace. He would smile, unruffled by the stresses he was under, content just to be with us.

Physically and emotionally my father seemed very distant, yet with compassion. He had a heavy heart. Once again he had to be separated from us, for study purposes. He had to requalify for his engineering degree, returning to university in his late '30s. He worked his way to designing roads and bridges in Australia.

Everyone loved my father for his gentle, kind and humble nature. On the way to the beach on the bus, he would proudly say, "These are the police toilets I cleaned."

He described to us how, during the times he was studying, he'd had to share a room with three slovenly men who were constantly intoxicated.

He was kept awake at all hours with their bodily noises. He tolerated this for three years, only getting to see us once a month.

My father instilled in me the ethics of loyalty, steadfastness and hard work.

I saw my father comfort my mother whenever she became distressed, which was often. He would put his arms around her. He offered her gentle words of solace but she nervously pushed him away as if nothing could console her. She could not be comforted. She had post-traumatic stress after WWII bombs fell around her during her teenage years in Russia and Germany. Also, she grieved the separation from her parents, who were not permitted to join her in Australia.

My father would withdraw emotionally and physically. He looked so alone. If I approached my father he would never communicate his pain verbally. But I could see his sadness. He kept it inside. I never saw my father show anger towards my mother.

Whenever my mother yelled at him, he responded with a quiet spirit. I saw he loved her. Once I saw my father cry bitterly. He broke down and sobbed. He stood alone, unaware I was observing him. He thought I was asleep.

My father stood by me in trials, as much as he could.

He was a true family man.

I remember when we moved into a huge two-story house, designed and built by an architect who had built it for himself. My father scraped layers of enamel-green paint off the bathroom walls. It took weeks. Every weekend he worked on the house. My mother had her own job, so was rarely at home.

I saw my father standing alone. Yet, there was a strength and contentment that shone through him.

People, including workmates, loved my father. He, in turn, had a gracious respect for all people. He had suffered hurt and persecution from the war years. Initially, upon arrival, we were treated badly by some Australians.

My father's office had been upgraded from a tin building in the CBD to a prestigious location with a plush office boasting spectacular water-views. It took my breath away when I came upon this sight.

Since he was now Chief Civil Engineer, my father was given the best desk at the wall, nearest and facing these views. As I looked around, while my father discussed a project, a lady came to me. She presented herself with a cheery smile. Slim, with a neat, simple dress. She said, "Your father gave me this desk. The best desk. I told him how I would love to have a desk facing the view. Your father said, you may take my desk and I'll take yours. He now has this desk here in the middle of the room. He is such a lovely man.

So kind."

Later, I questioned why he did the swap. He said, "She loved the views and I am happy sitting where I am. Besides, I have too much work to do to spend time looking at the views."

I saw him graciously agreeing to my mother's every request.

My father did the shopping and cooking, sometimes with me, but most often alone. The shopkeepers knew him and they always welcomed his cheery, generous nature. Happy dialogues flowed as he purchased our groceries.

Papa was consistent in his loyalty to us and to my mother. Many women wanted him but he declined them with kindness. Although my mother opposed my ballet and piano lessons, he stood against her decision and helped me. My father paid for these lessons himself.

My father found and accompanied me to Sunday School only for the first two Sundays. After that, I took myself. Each week, I counted the days and could not wait. I lived for Sunday School. The teachers showed kindness to all the children. Here I felt free to be me. I was accepted, not isolated from anyone else, in an environment where love and kindness flowed. I was learning about Jesus. I felt I belonged there. I loved learning and mixing with the other children.

Later, I was asked to sing in the church choir. Only a few selected children were asked to perform with the "big people's choir".

Though I longed for my mother to come and see me perform with the choir, she never did. My father came along to hear me sing as often as he could.

Separated from my mother at birth and raised for six years by my grandparents (after which I never saw my grandparents again), I developed a profound sense of loss. I was bullied at my school. When I tried to confide in my mother, she couldn't cope. My problems seemed trivial compared to what she had been through in the war.

My father too, had his heartaches. He became withdrawn. Most of the time he was working. He was like an apparition, hardly present in body or spirit. Yet he kept the home going. If I needed any practical things such as school books or uniform, Papa would organize that for me. He hardly ever spoke harshly to anyone. Yet I felt he was too quiet. I withdrew from his presence. He couldn't even hug me. We both shared the pain of isolation, unable to communicate our thoughts to each other.

I spent endless days going through as in a maze or a fog, getting nowhere, until I felt my father never existed. He kept on his path, never wavering. My father would never challenge my mother's behavior. He was of a gentle disposition. Yet, even when he was away from me I felt his presence of goodness.

One day while my father was upstairs, he overheard my screams.

I was about to be assaulted in my own home by someone who was a stranger.

Papa grabbed this fellow, shook and yelled at him, then threw him out of the house. My father took me in his arms and comforted me. I had never seen my father sob with so many tears, like rainfall flowing down his cheeks. He was so upset. He showed an anger I'd never witnessed before in his life. Nor had I ever heard him swear.

Appalling as this incident had been, in some ways my worst moment became my salvation, showing me the depth of my father's love. I'll never forget how he defended me. When my father eventually died of a heart attack, I held onto this.

His passing was at a time when I myself was critically ill.

I prayed fervently to the Lord, to bring someone who would care for me and love me for who I was. Within two weeks, my prayer was answered.

My soon-to-be husband, an Australian, helped me through this devastating time.

We clicked immediately over our shared common values around the love of God and children.

Eventually, I confessed I had been praying for someone to look after me and love me for myself. He admitted he had been praying for someone who genuinely needed him and loved him. We both believed our union was a divinely appointed miracle of God.

Very soon after we met, my husband encouraged and guided me to receive the Lord Jesus Christ into my heart. Initially I hesitated. I could not understand how a man, Jesus, could be God.

My husband loved me so much that he wanted, above all, for me to receive this gift. I remember so clearly the moment that I stepped out in faith and believed. Our marriage, from the start, was based on a relationship with God and each other. My husband taught me the scriptures and we regularly prayed together. He encouraged me to learn scripture verses by heart. Often these come to my mind when going through a trial, to help and strengthen me.

From the moment I met my future husband, until the day he died, he was constant in his love for me. If anything, his devotion grew over time. Under my husband's tender care, over ten years, I was brought back to good health. That, along with the love of our extraordinary children, and our faith in God, healed me.

He had a great sense of humor, and could turn a difficult situation around. This enabled us to overcome many hardships. He showed me how to trust in the Lord during difficult and seemingly impossible situations.

He was my Good Samaritan.

Even when my husband was in great pain before he died, he always encouraged me to trust in God and to never give up, no matter what. He was concerned about mine and our children's welfare above himself.

Two weeks prior to his death, he said to me, "Katarina, whether I live or I die, it will all work out for your good and for mine, and everything is for His glory. Keep on trusting in the Lord. With so much love in his eyes, he then said, "If I die, if you ever you meet a man who loves you and you love him, please get married."

As a child, I began to write into a book that became my best friend. This was my secret book, unknown to anyone. From here on in, I kept diaries for the rest of my life. Apart from teachers at school, as a child and young adult I had been given no encouragement to draw or write.

My husband recognized all of my talents and gave me much encouragement to use them. He would clean the house, make dinner and bring me a cup of tea while I painted. He bought me art paper, pencils, watercolors and charcoals.

One day he came in with a beautiful wooden box. Opening it, I marveled at the many colors, tones and the sheer number of the pastel sticks inside. I took a sensual delight in these art materials, touching and smelling them with great excitement. I felt magnetized to use them. Art paper followed a few days later. From this encouragement I sketched out my very first pastel pictures of live chooks and roosters.

When I wrote stories and poems and stuffed them into drawers, my husband became frustrated, since he wanted me to get my work out into the world.

He would be very pleased to hold this in his hand, my first published book, containing my original poems, short stories and illustrations. One of my husband's most cherished wishes has been granted.

I had never thought to publish my work for the sake of my own ego, but I have felt the urge to share in life what I have learned to encourage others.

I have come through many trials through trials and hardships by the grace of God. I am thankful He has allowed me to be broken, so that his light will shine out from me for his Glory, for his kingdom's sake. This is the joy that enables me to rise above all the dross and hurts, giving me confidence, peace and the desire to share His love with others. Life continues to present ongoing challenges. I see these as stepping stones to my growth, where my faith in Him has only grown stronger and I can be thankful for the lessons my enemies have taught me. So I have learned, and continue to learn to give thanks and praise for these.

I've realized I can create something beautiful through Him and for Him. There is a continued opportunity for character to develop through gratitude and learning to forgive. By accepting the consequences for my mistakes and sins, repentant, through God I am forgiven. This sets us free to live at peace even among our enemies. I am still being perfected. The Lessons continue to made me grow stronger in my faith in God through the Lord Jesus Christ

Acknowledgments

To the living God and to my late husband, I owe you both my life.
To those family members I cherish, past and present, you have given me riches beyond measure. To my teachers, friends and those who showed me kindness throughout my life, you know who you are. I am so grateful.

Thank you to Cambridge University Press:

Extracts from the Authorized Version of the Bible (The King James Bible), the rights in which are vested in the Crown, are reproduced by permission of the Crown's Patentee, Cambridge University Press.

Lastly, thank you to Stuart Innes, for his delicate photography that has faithfully rendered, in digital format, my original illustrations.

Introduction

In this book, ***Diary of a Passionate Poet: Beauty, Love and Hope in an Ordinary Life***, Katarina B. Viktor has observed with an eagle eye everyone around her, analyzing the minutiae of everyday life, from the mundane through to the extraordinary. She can see the splendor of nature in an ant or a blade of grass, or indeed, in a human that others would deem invisible.

With an artist's eye, a deep faith in God and love of family, Katarina has elevated the simple daily acts, to illuminate their meaning and true significance.

Viktor senses the poignancy and drama behind routine occurrences which form the glue that connects us in everyday life, while most of the world has blinkers on.

This book delves into universal themes, aspects of life that elevate us, grind us down, crack us apart and unite us in the warm glow of love and belonging. At those times she has reached rock bottom, it is the inspiration Viktor finds in God, Art and Family that have pulled her through. If the drudgery of life is beating you down, you can find a gentle solace here.

A Dancer's Waltz

A Dancer's Waltz

Lotus flower from the artist's watercolor palette
With fragrances oozing from this perfect sculpture.
Soft pinks merging into creams and greens
Embraced by warmth of sunlight's rays.
Gliding across on life giving waters
Where insects and beetles busy at work
See the rippleless lines these flowers make.
Strong, fine and clear.
Like skater's blades upon a fresh made block of ice.

This sight of lotus flowers,
Is like dancers in a waltz
Joined in Heaven's embrace.
Open, giving, strong,
Swaying bodies that command
The very breath of life be still.
Dance caught up with songs of angels.
Steps in perfect rhythmic beat.
Peace entwined in colors made by the Creator's Hand
Blends into ecstasies with tones of love.

Like ribbons flowing
Gently weaving into steps
Upon grasses green, soft to the touch
Sprouting beneath the feet.
As foreigners from a war torn, barren place
Arriving to a peaceful land.

All the wonders of the heavenly realm
Are fused as one.
Legs outlining petal shapes.
Spaces fill with varied hues – purples, creams, pinks and reds.
Bodies gliding, darting, smoothly weaving patterns.

The dancers' feet melt into velvet clouds.
No hardened floors can stop them now.
All barriers broken
Set free to leap in faith.
To laugh and glide
Like giant birds across vast oceans soar
In freedom find contentment here.
And as the waltz comes to the end
The lines they've made,
That beauty will be forever etched.
A painted masterpiece by God.

I watched this dance.
My soul's enriched.
Lotus flowers blossom on my mind.

On a Trampoline

Dedicated to all children

I'm a bird flying free.
Blue skies, soaring high on soft-breath winds
Gliding and smiling. Living is good.

I'm a puppy, soft to cuddle.
Fur so warm. I'm wanted.

I'm anything I want to be.

Bouncing, jumping high into space.
Open air. Down! I grip the earth.

You're a star or maybe an airplane.
And when you crash, we fall,
Join our hands and laugh.

Most of all I am me.
Unique and special. Just a one-off
Yet linked to you.
Living soul.
Loved.

I am a gift.
Beautiful.
Like a bird in soaring flight.

A Social Dance

Laughter, smiles,
Appearances of sophistication.
Superficial conversations
Fascinated by their own reflections.

There is no want for knowledge
Of the pain that lies within.
The very breath of life.

Souls broken
Crying out for kindness.
No remorse.
Hardened vessels
Filled with self.
To satisfy and fill with affluence
So squeeze compassion for another out.
The balance lost.

To have and to receive is good.
Why keep wealth to oneself, not allowing it to overflow?
Then another's heart is bathed in loving kindness,
Strengthened and restored.
It's self-deceptive
And will not give nor keep the happiness
We all seek.

It is in giving that we receive.
A secret that is open.
Free for all to have.
To hold.
What wealth we then can carry in our souls.

When a soul breaks out from this rigid mould
It is as though a blanket woven
From the strands of clouds
Is comforting the earth, the life,
With gentleness and love.
To share
Explore
Take an interest in one another.
And if there is pain
Reach out to give a hand.
The giving soul is a rare and beautiful gem.
Who lives not only for themselves
Who sees it is part of the Creation
Made by God.
To love, nurture and maintain.

The Game

The Game

I saw a little boy, perhaps three years of age
Walking with his mother pushing baby in a pram.
It was windy.

As she strove to push the tiny child
The little boy lagged behind.
Forlorn and lost, and rather pale he looked.
When suddenly he began a dance.
A little private jig – his own.
Dreaming…

Imagining to be a pirate in charge of the great seas.
Or could he be exploring lands unknown?
I stood and watched, delighting in his play.
And then he spied a smallish branch
Tipped with green and withered leaves.
He plucked it from the ground, unseen by adult eyes.
And then began to swirl it round and round.
Above, beneath him

Like a bird or plane, exhilarated, he danced in joyous flight.
I noticed that his sullen face had changed immediately to a rosy hue.
His lifeless hair stood out in proud array.
A smile that beamed showed pearly teeth
He danced a while unnoticed by his mother.
In frivolous ecstasy
Transported to another realm.

A land where children play.
A land where freedom has the key, unlocking soul.
No criticisms, no judgments or animosities are here.
Where dreams are born and built upon creations.
Heaven made in children's minds.

Where fairies play, and flowers dance.
Where blades of grass are forests in a strange land.
Where elephants and tigers roam in peace
At one with themselves and the world.

Where imaginations are protected.
And energies soar high.
And give the children special places
And make each one dearest and unique and very strong.
Secure in this world of make believe.
Heaven sent by God – Creator of the universe and humankind.

I stood, enjoying this array of joy.
From just a little child
So special did it bring to me
Memories sweet tasting
Of joy and love, peace and freedom
That this world has in its grasp
And yet with cares, strife and sorrows
Can be choked away
And leave a barren ground.
Deserted – not a living soul or nature's beauty found.
I stood, and did not want to move.

Then! As the little boy danced closer to his Mum
He smiled affectionately to her
As if to say, "Come share in this wonderful place I have.
Play with me, surround yourself with simple laughter.
And dream your dream.
I've found a very special place away from cares and strivings.

Away from worries about the mortgage
Away from the business of daily chores.
Don't be sad, come dance and play with me."

The mother, looking hard at her little boy
A tired face revealing the never ending frustrations of her life
Snatched the branch away from him.
And with deliberate motion of disgust
Threw the little branch away from her
As far as she could.

I saw the leaves tremble through the wind
Rubbish, unwanted, alone, lifeless the branch lay
The child and his dream – separated.
By an unexplainable abyss.
Lost, forever here.

The branch lay quivering in the wind alone.
Like a forsaken piece of puzzle.
And the child gasping at the reality of his loss,
In shock, bewilderment and grief.
The little boy confused, began to cry.
His precious dream, his play was crushed.

I saw he tried to reason with his Mum
And then I saw his face return to sullen, pale
No more smile or laughter
The light that shone had been extinguished
And as he walked silently beside his mother dear
Obedience had won.

How sad I felt
I so much longed to share this freedom with the child.
Encourage him to be the tree
With branches blowing in the wind

Or be the bird or plane or pirate that he be.
I left this scene and walked on home.

As my hands swished through my bag to find my keys.
The little boy, one hand in mum's.
Passed by me gazing sadly and lovingly upon me.
I waved to him, mum oblivious to our connection.
He walked along trapped by this world's sadness and heavy load.
I saw a loving mother who does her best
Encumbered with the cares of daily life
Who cannot see the play, dreams and creativity of her child.
God bless them both.

May this child blossom with God's love for him.
And bless his mum that she finds rest and joy
In living, dancing and playtime with her precious child.
I walked to my door, with sad, ponderous thought
I've done, at times, the very same when mine were young.
Consumed with busyness of the day
And all the chores that must be done.
How oft I worried so unnecessarily.
And fell into that trap of lies.
Oh, blessed are they who can see
That love and youthful joy
Are the essences of life in living here on Earth.

Childhood Blessings

Will I remember when I'm grown
That my mother had my room tidy?
Shall we remember that our clothes were always clean?

No! We will remember the times
You held us close.
Our hearts beat together.
You stroked our backs.

We knew we were so precious to you.
You gave us self-esteem and security.
So little condemnation, so little criticisms were received.
We remember how often you told us that you loved us.
Your open smiles
Laughter in your eyes that shone with love.

Will we remember the social graces you taught us?
And wash our hands before our meals?

Mostly we remember
The times we sat upon your knees
And all the books you read to us.
The warm embraces.
The times you showered us with your patience and with love.
The walks, talks and picnics that you gave to us.
We were so special to you, even from the time of our conception.

Later, you gave us your time when we had things to chat about.
When we fell over and bruised our knees
You were there with a kiss and a smile to make us better.
And when we needed to talk over life's challenges
You listened.

So we overcame and became stronger.
We grew and developed into healthy adults.
We learned and saw God's love for us through you.
That we were created to give you joy
And you, to joy in us.
To share Christ's Great Love together.
To have a family so special.
To know we were created in heaven
To be a gift to you
And in gratitude I give thanks to God
That we were given as a mother and father— you.

And after playtime
Having had so much fun.
Covered in grime
We'd run indoors.
You'd hug us.
Seeing only our smiles.

You would take off our muddy clothes.
And we would have a fun bath time.
Fed well and tired
We would feel a gentle kiss
Upon our brows.

As we were laid into our beds
Angels surrounded around us
And we fell asleep so peacefully.

You worked hard to make our lives the best you could.
How often you put away our toys
And taught us with patience to do the same.
Such games we played.
In the wonder of enchanted imagination, we developed more.

We've grown into well adjusted, happy, living souls.
And with this gift we bring to you.
Our joy of just "to be".
Growing to be the best we are and can do.
With thanks to you for giving us
The freedom based on Love.

A Blade of Grass

The Earth cries out to meet you, Lord.
I see the desert sands.
Arms outstretched from pools of water
From a parched land.
I need your love, Lord.

Heal me, as a green blade.
Pierces and writhes out of red dust.
What strength it shows as it grows.
In spite of harsh, hard land.
Here it grows – alone.
Rejected.

Yet your sun rays life-giving light and warmth
Upon the delicate green.
Vulnerable it is.

Love and caring surrounding this breath of life
Sustains its growth.
Though unnoticed
It is beautiful.
Beloved of God.

(Written while sitting alone, listening to music that provoked me to
write).

Lady in the Red Dress

Unsure, yet in sophisticated gait
She stands, smiles and moves her body,
Lithe, to the music beat.
Her dress lays snug and smooth
Upon her trim and rounded body.
Pearls around her neck
Fall into her large, exposed cleavage.

She appears totally contented
The beat of the music thrills her senses.
She gives a flirty glance
And nudges her husband
To dance with her.
She longs to be held
To share this moment of freedom – with him.
She loves her man.

He stands beside her
Stiff, embarrassed, motionless.
No tender embrace
No sweet word to her.
Disconnected.

She stands disillusioned
Her face now showing many lines upon it.
Youth has flown.

She moves away from him to other company.
Her moment, her dream that could have been,
Is gone.

Solace

Alone I wept so silently
I hadn't got a friend
To tell my fears
Or gentle hands to brush away my tears.

I'm feeling sad, so frail
And even scared
Of living in this wretched world.
Such misery is crawling everywhere.
Like termites, it does chew.
In forms of apathy and Godlessness.

Cold, steely hearts.
It leaves behind its trail of self.
Uncaring webs are woven
Where no harmony brings.
Its only end is death.
And death that is its prey.
It must go on.
For in the light they'd be exposed.
Like x-rays of their sin.
And sin is what they choose.

I sit here, grieving and so confused.
So lost and so alone.
Then you softly touch my hand.
And gently kiss my brow.

And ask if I could let you in.

You sup with me.
And I with you.
Such treasure, splendor you do share with me.
My shattered dreams and hopes restored.
My thoughts and pains forgotten.

For what are these earthly trials
Compared to knowing you, My Lord?
Sitting at your feet my spirit leaps for joy,
In wonder and in ecstasy.
This gift you bring and freely give to me
I marvel in your presence
That Thou O God, the Great "I AM"
Should choose this little one
To be Your Friend
And make a comfort home
In me.

A pitiful, simple body
That's scarred and marred
Twisted and warped within.
You choose to sup with me.
The feasting's just begun,
And goes on eternally.

Out of God's Will

Rushing, panic, anxious
Was my life
'Til I yielded it to You.
To take my feeble mind
And then I gave my will to You.
To do with as You will.

And so I found my answer to peace and happiness.
To seek and trust You and do Your Will. Obey Your word.

Let me walk with You.
Guide me through all life's despairs and
Trials that come my way.
See them more as challenges to break and shape me
That I may grow to be more like You.

Though this refining is very painful
It's the only way that You can cause the selfish "I" to die.
Turn me into a precious jewel
That sits upon your crown.

For satisfying "I" with its greed,
Selfish and unloving ways
Blocks the flow from me to You and You to me.

"I" must die, so that You in me should live.
Then, a happy life
In You, complete.

The Perfect in the Imperfection

The Perfect in the Imperfection

A beautiful vase
Made with caring hands.
Carefully, lovingly
Turning a lump of insignificant clay
Into a beautiful shape.

As the wheel turns
He thinks of how it will look and feel
And how it will take pride in someone's home.
How it will be admired by all.

He enjoys this time of play
And then the firing in the "high temp" oven.
Then, an intricate and stunning design
With glazes of the purest colors
Painted on with care.
A final glazing, and a last firing.

It is done.
Absolute delight.
Just perfect.
Unique.

So rare, so beautiful.
His heart is filled with gratitude and pride.
That an object of such beauty,
Of such worth

He has created from a lump of clay.
Upon a shelf it stands admired by many.
The sunlight captures its beauty of form and color.
Light and shadows add life to this Master's creation.

Then, from the stand it falls to the ground.

Shattered.
Broken.
In many pieces it lays.
This creation
So perfectly made
So rare, is now worthless.
He stands with gasping breath
Unable, for some time, to move.

To see this Perfection
So broken
In many pieces
All his work
Destroyed.

With an almost unbearable, aching heart
He moves with reverence
Collecting the broken pieces of the pot.
With tears welling
He makes a move to throw the shards into a bin.

Suddenly, he stops and thinks
To glue these pieces back to reconstruct the pot.
With care and time, he does.
Beauty can once more be seen.
With cracks all through this beautiful pot
It stands.

Perfect in its imperfection.

Just like us.
We can be shattered.
God allows this brokenness to seep within our souls.

So break us
Make us more like God
Loving, gentle, kind, forgiving
Standing up for justice.

We trust and obey the Lord Jesus Christ.
With gratitude in our hearts that we are so loved
We give thanks in prayer
Walking on the path of Christ the Risen Savior
So that in our imperfection
Through our cracks of human failings
God's light, God's love shines through.
The Perfect in the Imperfect.

Diary of a 15-year-old Boy

The sun was setting. A soft mist lingered in the air.

The boy ran, puffing, excited. He had met his first love. They'd had their first quarrel and he had tried to patch it up. The confusion of puberty, and this rejection, was a major event in his life. This was a serious matter to be resolved at all costs.

Nobody understood. He had to solve it by himself, alone.

His mind was already crowded with many thoughts, plans and expectations. He was young, yet shouldered adult responsibilities because no-one would show him affection, give him a gentle word, or their time.

When he reached his gate, he was warm. Perspiration formed a tiny layer on his skin. His hands were large. He was deep in thought. As he opened the door, a soft, grey mist came from his mouth.

He did his homework, though lessons, books and learning were far from his mind. He had to do the work, and diligently set out to complete it.

He often dreamed of kissing her, gently then passionately.

He thought he'd like to dance with her and be with her forever. He imagined swimming with her or cheering her at her tennis match.

How lovely was her light brown hair, with eyes that spoke so intimately to him. Her smile was kind and her words were soft, always soothing. What joy it was to be with her, to hold her hand, to talk, to laugh.

He wanted to plan a life with her. To be alone with her and grow old together.

He was confused.

A boy so young, yet in the throes of maturing. He had his own identity, ideals and dreams. His parents did not know of these. He kept to himself. He never shared much with his mother and father.

And so he grew, in secret.

Diary of a 30-year-old Man

One day, he left home and got married.

Then, the reality of life struck him. Again he felt confused, this time lost. He stumbled for the careless freedoms, the laughs he had found in long, lost youth. He recalled caresses in the breeze, the times of no responsibilities when they could do as they pleased, no-one bothered them, and sunshine and smiles were free.

The bills piled up. She began to lose her happy natured ways. Her face grew tense as biting words left her lips. Anger set in and both began to loathe the other. Each went their separate ways, rejected and disillusioned. Paradise was gone forever. They were alone without another.

Chores

Despair hit me.
There's lots to be done.
I don't know where to start.

I pray.
You tell me, "Seek my Word."

It's just too hard for me right now.
And I'm so tired too.
Your helping hand is always here, I know
To see me through.

Yet in my anguished solitude
My children must be nurtured.
I've been neglecting them, I know.
What mother am I now?

I want to seek the pleasures of the day,
To laugh, to walk among the trees
And have sweet fellowship with people
And with Thee.

They are not here, all are gone.

I'm so alone.

Lord help me to be just content with Thee.

To look to you,
And do my jobs.
With gladness in my heart.

I know then as I put my trust in you
You'll do the rest
And make my life complete.

A Good Night Out

Last week, a friend of mine explained what had happened to her the night before. This incident made me chuckle. As a parent, I could relate.

This is her story, in her own words:

My husband had been away for three long weeks. He arrived and took us out for dinner.

"How nice," I thought, "a break from the mundane chores I've done all day at home."

How lovely to relax, enjoy the meal and have a quiet conversation.

I craved peace, away from all rowdy play and high pitched chatter.

While waiting for the orders to be served, my daughter yelled out exciting things about gnomes and space creatures.

Her brother told her to be quiet. My head began to throb.

The order arrived.

My daughter grabbed for some delicious morsel. A glass of water spilled. It trickled down my legs. I saw myself leaving, heading for the safety of home.

We ate and enjoyed the pizzas and the soup.

A little squabble broke out between the kids. Yet, in my head, it seemed like a war.

My husband didn't talk a lot to me. I found solace in my son. He told me a funny tale while his Dad got ice-cream for our little daughter— to compensate. Because, guess what? She didn't like *that* pizza! Ham and pineapple is the one she likes, not salami, pepperoni and olives.

She hardly ate her pizza but shoveled in the gelato.

As we walked back to the car, our little girl suddenly stopped. She vomited, right down the back of my black skirt and onto the footpath.

I felt a squelchy substance inside my shoe and again my legs felt wet.

I preferred the water!

My daughter was grizzling. Her brother yelled out, "Yuck!"

I noticed my husband had also been sprayed.

We made eye contact, and started to laugh. My husband grabbed a napkin and tried to wipe us down, but it was futile. He turned to comfort our daughter instead.

Children are so priceless! I looked at her, and him, my two precious ones, and thanked the Lord for the joy they bring. This is what family life is all about. They'll not be little for long. Our boy is almost 13. Yes, I had a good night out with the ones I love safe and well.

Could I have wished for anything better?

Maybe a "cuppa" in a quiet little spot.

The Man in the Park

Young yet old,
Face lined with wrinkles, deep.
Sitting on the bench.
Forlorn.

Lost in a wilderness, with no other soul to care.
All his possessions lay bare by his side.
A battered trolley with a missing wheel,
Looks as though it had some style in days gone by.
Stained blankets peering out from it.

His shirt is simple yet not dirty
And his trousers just hang but don't belong to him.

As I pass by, I stop a moment to give him a smile.
He looks at me.
My heart stops as my being crumples up.
A longing grips my soul.

Where is he going?
Where did he come from?
Does anyone miss him?
What is his purpose in life?

I pass by, respectful for not to break his stagnant silence.
With a saddened heart I go on my way.
I walk another lap of the park.

After 15 minutes, I round the bend.

He's still there.
At home – park bench, trolley and a bag
 Containing all of his worldly possessions.
 No-one would care to steal from him.
He does not notice me this time.
 The man picks up a black hair comb.
He looks down, as he runs it through his hair.
 I notice there is a good amount of black hair upon his head.
He is not old in age,
 But sorrow has dealt him a hand.

The Skylark Soaring

The Skylark Soaring

Rising to clouds,
After treading the weary ground,
With wings like a drill,
Working through concrete.
Strong and unrelenting,
Soaring upwards,
'Til only you become a speck
Against that wash of blue.
Clear and vast.
With only clouds to decorate your scene.

So free,
Alone you soar.
Above the trees,
Majestic hills and mountains.

The thrills of your voice
Like diamonds.
Clean, clear, cutting through the air.
Falls upon a land that cries.
The pity of your voice
Closes it with hope.

Higher you soar
Like a waterfall
Filled with jewels and gems,
Voice of colors.

Trills, as crystal breaking crystal.
Clear, strong and piercing
Melodies that no composer has made.
Inviting me to partake
In your joy of life.

Are you the speck, or me?
Your notes fall upon my face,
My body.
Cleansing me of all the trials
That life brings.

In your voice
I hear the sounds of hope.
Each note vibrates,
Releasing droplets in saturated hues.

The orchestra is set.
Intense,
Strong.

The air,
The universe
Melodious.
Of songs so rare
Rich and warm.
That only angels
Of the Lord can sing.
That drip on me
Like flowing petals.

Dedicated to My Husband

Dedicated to my Husband

I smell a rose
I see the soft lush color
I feel the velvet robe
First on my fingertips.

In awe I touch the petals
Then bury my cheek in the flower
Like the bosom of a mother's tender love.
Embracing me
Powerfully!

Dewdrops falling from this flower
Kiss me.
Refreshing me with hope.
You showed me God's love,
My dear kind, gentle, patience caring husband.
My soul mate.
Soothing, refreshing my mind.
Giving me power to live, love and
Trust in God's Love for us.

Inhaling life-giving breezes.
The memories of you and me,
Soft grasses beneath our feet
Being protected by the canopies of leaves above.
Soothed by cooling raindrops
Hugged by the tallest mountains.

Encouraging me to fly on the wings of eagles.
Knowing we are loved by our Creator
We can, and will go on, in joy and laughter.
Strong to do God's will, not ours
And love as God loves us!
Forever I'll be very grateful that God blessed me with you.

Sunset at Royal Botanic Garden Sydney

A plane flying past the Sydney Harbour Bridge
Along a ribboned band of gold
That turns vermillion and magenta red.
Curtain backdrops
To a sleepy traffic
On the black ink-etched bridge
Dotted with jeweled gold and silver lights.
The clouds stand proud
Like mountains, strong, secure,
Made of pure gold.

Mountains forged out of a sea
Holding treasures deep within the craggy cliffs
That time holds still.
The very breath of ancients holding stories.

Lives woven with
Threads, paralyzed
Forever, moments of time.
Never ending, never moving, never changing.
Beauteous treasures and peace.
A glimpse of Eternity with God.

Horizon and Sailing Boat

Straight line
Horizon
Separating soft, blue skies
With the melting white of clouds
Like marshmallows over sizzling fires.

Dripping softly into blue Ultramarine line
Below rests cobalt stripes
Merging once more into Ultramarine.
Soft and heavy hued stripes alternate
Of cobalt and ink blue, cerulean and greens.

Far away, almost touching gently the horizon
A sailing boat stands still
As though in wonderland is lost.
Which way to go?
I sit and wonder on this majestic sight.

To smell and see and feel
The presence of the Peace of God
Of dreaming, adventures, bold and rare.

Travels into other lands
The peace, joys, exhilarations,
The mind that beauteous creations can absorb.
Dreams of sitting in that little boat.
That picture, touching and being touched!

Nightingale—My Grandmother

Strong, clear notes
Throat expanded
Holding, owning treasures.

Golden threads of voice poured forth
In brilliant, radiant confidence.
In tune with sun and all creation.

With thanksgiving
To live and to love,
To reach the icy mountain tops
That melt to sunlit rivers below.

These notes of power
Lasting, enduring
Ever giving beauty
Are more precious than all the gold and rubies in the world.
Contained in one small bird
Each vein and fiber of her body
Tells me life is good.

To endure, to live through pain and hardships,
To soar above all trials.
Living, breathing,
Giving love and power.
Reveling in being wrapped in love's finest
Blends of silver and golden threads.

This statement of confident command.
Rejoicing in the very breath
Preceding life.
These powerful threads of notes of love
Freely flow,
Cannot be destroyed
Nor can they be contained.
They light the dimmest places
And reach the highest mountain tops.

The nightingale song will endure.
Rain will always clothe a shining leaf
And my grandmother's embrace will always be alive.

She held me close and I could feel the warmth of love.
Her beating heart showed me the power of life.
The nightingale and her
Show me how blessed I am
To see and know the Grace and Love of God.
I pray I can pass on this love to others.

The Gift

Ribbons, bands of pastel hues,
Pinks, blues, yellows,
Wrap loosely around my body.
Draping, long,
Each telling, each holding
Stories of my life.
I am made as a cocoon
Feeling safe, secure in this.
Yet I see all is meaningless

The good, the bad,
Mistakes, sins, triumphs, gifts, achievements.
Gains, losses, the loves, the apathies
Will seep away.
As water poured onto desert sands.
No value, no worth will hold.

The greatest music,
Symphonies of sublime beauty,
Paintings done by hands and minds of genius,
Brilliant architecture
That lives on long after the artist's death
Will also be dissolved.
No more exist.
Enduring only is the Love of God.
All else is meaningless.

The greatest artist with gifts that dazzle with awe
Has a meaningless life without the Love of God.

Only the gift of Love lives on.
The spirit and gifts are separate
The soul devoid of Love is already dead.
Yet the gift can live, encourage.
Be a springboard for love and joy to grow.

Yet even gifts one day will be no more.
As mortals giving and leaving gifts behind,
Rotting underground with tombstones planted.

With noteworthy sayings mostly forgotten,
Some remembered, revered, admired.
Thanked for leaving us with such beauteous gifts.
Music, art, inventions, kind deeds.
These gifts too one day will be no more.

All that will endure is Love.
As ribbons
Floating, flowing
Freely, wildly, lavishly
Into Eternity.

Only Love, the Lord Jesus Christ
Has meaning
In this wild, bizarre entanglement of life.
Complexities and tragedies, pains and struggles.
Self-strivings for happiness
The falls, despairs,
The rising up and challenges,
The triumphs, failings,

Feeling good, Feeling bad.
All are
And will one day be gone,
Meaningless.

Only love
Like ribbons
Will endure, without any seams.
Strong
Encircling and wrapping around this earth.
Good deeds done.
Where secrets will one day be revealed.
The pains and the tortures
Cruel deeds done. Good deeds done.
Hardships, rejections, fears, kindness,
Will be no more
And like the ribbon
That encircles me
Will take me, secure,
Home.
I will live in love
and love will live in me,
Forever.

The Sea

You provoke in me the passions of my youth.
My childhood days spent dreaming of fairytales and heroes.
Of myths, legends and scenes from outer space,
Of lying upon soft turf, laughter and rolling down green hills.
Of holding hands with brother and sister
And licking ice-creams.
Telling secrets and playing spy games,
Of being fairies and monsters,
Building cubby houses – safe, secret, creative play houses.

My body feels your velvet touch, wrapping itself around me tip to toe.
Tells me my troubles are few.
Your waves wash all over me.
I feel the comfort of this soft caress.
I am warmed and I welcome your sweet touch.

I laugh – I remember the days of my adolescence,
My romantic days of stolen kisses.
Warm embraces with soft endearing words from one who loves me deeply, when passions were aroused.
I feel as if I'm the most special, most wanted person on this whole earth.

Beauty looks full on at me.
I see myself as strong, beautiful and ecstatic to be me.
In youth I look fearlessly at you.

I wonder at your depth and beauty.
I feel such peace standing by your side.

Waves lapping at my feet. I had such problems a while ago.
How is it you can wash them all away?

Sweet conversation is had,
exchanging life and thoughts.

I look at my beloved.
"Would you, oh sea, seem all so good to me,
If I was not loved by him?"
He holds my hand,
A gentle embrace.

The sea and love go hand in hand.

Girl on a Swing

As a pendulum suspended in the air,
  What thoughts are going through your mind, my child?
Are they of love and joy, and pretty things,
  Of sweet expectations,
  Like the early morning dew from gentle rains?

As you sit there laughing with hair tied in large, satin bows,
Are you secure in your blanket of acceptance?
Have you received the affections you deserve,
  So your eyes can gleam with appreciation?
Of the shiny leaves your little feet can touch,
Of the pretend games of soaring as a bird
  Free in the cloudless blue sky?

Are your thoughts of daffodils and ice-cream,
And little friends to laugh and play with,
  Of blades of grass, soft and fresh to caress your little feet?
Of smiles of kind folks who pass you by,
And carousels and fairy floss?

Or are your thoughts of what you'd like it to be, and is not?
Of dark tunnels, strangers and despair?
Is there fear in your eyes?
Are you alone,
  To dream and to wonder at this life ahead of you?

Is your hair all matted and tangled?
Does anyone brush it with love?
Are the ribbons gone?
Is your face sad – little friends are gone?
Is the ice-cream and carousel for someone else?

Can the leaves and trees hear your sad request?
Does only the wind give you comfort with its caress?
Are the blades of grass all withered and yellow?
Do they prickle your tender little feet?

Little girl on a swing,
Take hope all is not lost.
You can dream of what life could be.
You'll gain strength on that swing,
As you feel God's love for you,
And know he is caring for you.

You'll learn not to be harsh, unkind and plain cruel.
To smile and laugh at what's good.
When you get off that swing,
"Go! Be free!"
Though the brush may cut at your feet.
Know that you are loved,
Find the beauty that abounds,
On this terrible earth that God made.
Be free, to know he cares for you,
With a love that surrounds and overflows through you.

You can give love,
Sow seeds of joy,
Wherever your blistered feet tread.

The Swallow and the Eagle

She sits upon still waters,
A speck upon the pond.
At peace and satisfied,
Fulfilled.

She made her nest,
Fed well her chicks.
They've flown to make a life their own.

Satisfied,
She contemplates her well done job.

Now she can gloat,
And float,
Wherever she desires.

Menu is her own.
Yet, she dreams to be an eagle,
and soar above the craggy cliffs.

Storm

Blues changing to blacks,
Noise to break our bones,
Screeching birds.
Safe,
Behind our wet, dark panes.

My Baby

His first smile.
  Sunshine,
  Grounded in Love,
Hope.

Grief—Loss of a friend

I cannot fly.
I cannot sing.
Grounded,
Forlorn,
Dazed.

I put my trust in God
And wait in hope
For my return to you.
My soul to fly again.

Joy.
Healing restored.
To my broken wing.

Night Walk to the Beach

Night Walk to the Beach

Walking in the night
Drops of rain
Refresh my face.
Nostrils pierced by the sting of cold air
Upon my soft, warm face.
Falling horizontally
With winds that bow.
The branches of big, old trees.
If a branch breaks, where will it fall?

The air is fresh at the beach front.
Not a soul can be seen or heard.
Just the spirits of people a few days ago,
Laughing and swimming in the sunshine.
Strolling in the evening near quiet waters
Breaking on the shores.

I am enraptured in this solitude
That entices me to stand and stare.

I am a speck in this vast landscape,
Magnetized to the ground.
Cannot move.

My breath pounds with my heart
In rhythm to the crashing waves ahead.

The moon and I, and solitude.
Crashing waves,
No artist could imitate.
Their sounds,
My breath.

I receive such treasure.
This marvel of creation
I sense, just for a moment.
This gift for me is given.
I am strengthened by God's love
To give again to all.

I am nothing,
Yet I have discovered,
Found this panoramic paradise,
A jewel to cherish
In my memory forever.
A soul alone
Yet not alone.
The moon, the sea, the rain, the blackness, the solitude.

Footsteps washed away where children played,
A few days before.

Conversation, laughter,
Frozen.
Thick line of blackness,
Stillness, and the moon.

I leave behind my feelings,
That I have marveled at,
And what I've seen before me now.

The beating, breathing of Creation,
Inviting me to take this peace,

To chew it slow,
And let it flow within my veins.

With every breath I cannot stop my pounding heart.
I leave the footprint of my breath upon the air.
I take with me the gratitude of what I have just held.
The moon has witnessed me in this.

I take with me the memory.
It is etched into my brain.
The moon smiles as I turn away,
And longing cradles me.

A blanket snug,
Where I belong
This piece of gold,
This solitude.

Louth—Christmas Day

You might think we're at a circus
Or the greatest drama play.
You might think we're in the desert
Or a 5-star hotel for a day.
But no, we're right here in an outback town
Staying with Flo and Ben,
Real honest, country folk.
Many a mile you'd go to find such treasured gems.

The township here looks sleepy
But life is full beneath the surface.

Flo is straight as dice.
She has an Aussie twang.
Says what she means,
Occasionally gets sharp.
She's on her feet most of the day
But laughter can be heard.
Though meals are served at any time
They're hearty and complete.
You may not look at her in the street
But the goodness of her heart
Would make anyone stop and take a leap.

Ben, the greasy shearer, is rough and ragged as can be.
But I've got to know him.

He's gentle as a lamb.
He knows the bush like the back of his right hand.

They are a pair,
Who love and hurt the same as anyone,
But they've also got a bit to give to outsiders passing by.

People here are rather quiet
'Til they get the beer into them.
Then they just talk about the doings in the town and bush.
They are obsessed with news and weather
The ins and outs can be thoroughly discussed.
Time stands still.

"Shot a 'roo last night for Bill's yabbie trap,
no trouble!"
"Saw a few black pigs as well."
I'd seen them too, crossing the red dusty road like two dark rocks
stuck in the middle of a dry, lonely country.

I find life here not dull at all.
The city folk could envy at this life.
People here are down to earth
Enjoying life with not much strife.

Most locals work very hard on stations near and far.
Friends of Flo and Ben's I've met are honest, simple folk who'd
Rather help than harm.

But Louth has part of my heart won to its rugged, rustic beauty.

The local pub is a pleasant, busy place.
Many passersby come and go, refreshed by Wendy's hospitality and
sparkling eyes. At the Christmas party, Wendy warmly welcomes
us. She is gracious.

Wendy must have worked and worked all day,
yet looks as fresh as dew. Soft warm air, with food so lovingly
prepared by her, with creative expertise.

The celebration, enjoyed by all, forms a pleasant memory.
In a gesture to the locals there was a party at the pub.
Parents rounded up their children, to join in the fun.
Bright-eyed, strong, youngsters sang carols with us.

As our voices rang out, I learned from them more,
God's love can be seen in happy faces such as these.
For one and all, Christ died to set us free
To live, and to love one another and thee.

Stan, a happy, carefree young man
Is champion to the kids
Can crack the whip with accuracy and speed.
I had a challenge at this craft –
Cracked it and got a fair sting on the buttock!

People here take others as they are
I've found acceptance easy here.
Life is slow alright. But dull? No way.
An accident on a motor-bike
One knee badly hurt
The other buttock and legs hurting bad.
It is the talk of all the town!

Word sure gets 'round here fast.
Jokes are made.
Friendships can be seen,
And pain like this goes on for days (even months)!
For pampering here is lapped and soaked up
Deep beneath the skin.

My hubby is in his element with medicine and bandages on hand.
He came prepared, all right.
Much fussing, scurrying and much business.
You'd think it were Central Square.

Then, after "yowls," growls and shouts,
First Aid has been applied, professionally.

Flo is run straight off her feet,
With "Mum, me leg's in pain!" screaming so loud
You'd think the war broke out!

What we remembered most about Louth
Was the warmth of our reception,
And Flo's homemade mayonnaise!
It was the centerpiece of the Christmas meal.
Everything was doused in it.
To this day I laugh when I think of it.

To a Linnet

Linnet
When you sing,
With trills so fine,
So intricate,
To show your skills.

With smoothest, gliding power,
Of notes so rare
In purity of tone.
So clear to reach the ears
Of heavenly angels,
And sing with them,
A harmony in chorus.

To color bush and sea,
and all therein
This land and sky.

Do you know
With every note you take
What it is to love,
And know the ecstasy and joy
Of being with your true love?

Do you know
The tender, sweet caresses

Of his fingertips
Upon your face and brow?

Do you know the warmth
When he holds you close?
Have you felt the beating of his heart
In loving surges,
One by one?

Have you known and felt
His endless love for you?
Passion that can never be extinguished,
An ever flowing river,
Love flows on for you?
Just like the notes you sing
Each day that flow and melt
Into distances that cannot be seen
And join with your heavenly choir.
Somewhere far off into that realm of Godly praise
That people just can't see.

But you, oh Linnet,
You can see
The gifts of Earth and Heaven,
That God has given you,
To capture and enjoy,
Unto Eternity.

Do you, Linnet know
The wonder of being joined to your lover?
To know that you are loved,
And that is all
For God is here embracing you,
And so you can grasp Christ's love, too.
Intoxicated by the warmth of just being.

Do you, Linnet, know
The depth of sorrow
When Spirit departs
And death makes ugly of it all for you?

Do you, Linnet, know what it is
To sit upon your bough and sing alone?
Disenchanted that your voice,
Now full of grief and sorrow
Carries its tune
In monotone drone
For miles unto the heavens.

Reaching down, his spirit comforts you
And now you can sing in harmony,
Once more with the heavenly angels.
Delighted in the knowing
That you are not alone,
But united
With him and the Living God.

Do you know the freedom of being forgiven
And Loved by God?
Freedom,
To love, forgive, and
Receive love?
The joy of singing out of
Contentment.
Surrounded by the peace and beauty of
God's love for all.

I believe Linnet, you do!

A Harsh Beauty

The land with yellow-red earth,
Sprawled out mile upon mile,
Deserted.
My footprints clearly visible behind me.
Strands of yellow-like thin ribbons,
Meticulously placed
To outline the red, forgotten land.

This deserted plain
Extends beyond what eye can see.
The sun is hot and fierce.
The sandy grains are coarse.
My feeble knees grow weak.
I feel I cannot go much further.

Yet the sky is cloudless.
Red, yellow and blue I see
And me,
Alone.

Yet I feel empowered.
This desolate place has gripped me.
A beauty of the same
Simplicity and nothingness
Invades this place with power.
With mysteries of comfort,
Devoid of the cruelties of people.

Hard hearts,
Betrayals,
Murderous and selfish ways.
I feel at one with this place.

Then a dance of light before me is displayed,
Majestic,
Powerful,
Commanding.
I'm captivated by this miraculous sight.
A flower blooming
All alone.

At once I feel akin
The sun's rays kissing
The open petals.
They receive the radiant warmth of God's love.
They smile
Knowing they live
In his constant, ever giving, never ending love.

The sun's light shimmering
Like ballerinas dancing on their toes.
His love is here to stay, unwavering, unconditional.

So this flower thrives
Through harsh storms and rains
Through droughts and floods it blooms,
Strengthened through life's adversities,
Shining God's light, for me to see.

It speaks encouragement of the loveliness of God
The stem can bend,
Be flexible,
Because The Master has his way.

These roots by him are firmly planted in the soil.
Through many trials and testing
The flower has endured
Lifted up towards the heavens.

Wedding Day

For though dost love me as a rose
Whose crushed velvet petals
Ooze the sweet perfume of love,
To fill the nostrils
And intoxicate the heart.

Oh love that with your velvet touch
Caress the innermost of my heart.
It weeps no more but leaps with joy.

Each time the fragrance of your name it spells,
I see your beauty waiting patiently for me,
While I am rushing doing this or that.

The joy that this, our Lord, should bring to me,
That, in completeness, we may live our lives in harmony.
Caring, sharing with sweet thoughts of love,
And with respect, serve another's needs.

You came into my life when struggles were so large.
I was discouraged and, with a gentle touch, you took my hand.
I know the Lord was with me, though people had betrayed me.
God, through you, wiped away my tears,
So we can tread the Lord's path, and do God's will together.

Vows

As the gentle winds caress my face
So you with each embrace show me the joy to live.
And when I've this and that to do,
And don't know quite just where to move,
You sit and patiently wait for me.

Your love is freedom just to be
I pause and marvel how the Lord brought you to me
Beyond our prayers God has answered so much more.
I feel the softness of the grass and smell the roses at our feet,
I know the love that Christ has given us,
He's one in us, and we are one in him.

Like a rose, life has its thorns
So when the thorns do come our way
We will not wither
Nor fade away.
Your soft words cause me to stop
And meaning floods my soul—
The love of freedom,
Just to be accepted,
The love that God has brought to us,
That we can share together.

I cannot help but laugh and sing,
As this jewel,
This beauty that is you,

Is given as a priceless gift to me
And I to you.

When the bitter storms of life may come
Me, you and the Lord will be one
We'll rise victoriously.
Our love in time for one another
Will keep us safe and strong.

Just Like You

To be loved and accepted is the thrill of life for me.
See! I am an ordinary person
Given an extraordinary life.
I want to live it to the full.

Some think I am disabled,
That I cannot feel pain or joy,
That I have no tears to cry,
Nor be grateful for a smile.
Many think I have no dreams,
That life is meaningless
Because I am restricted to a chair,
Just because I walk with a twisted gait.

My mind is sound.
I can see the beauty of the trees
And feel the calmness in an olive grove.
I delight in smelling flowers
And scrunching autumn leaves.
I feel,
I think,
I observe.
Just like others do.
I see that "normal"
Is to love and be loved.

Could "handicapped" mean
Those who do not wish to see the truth
In loving and being loved?
They live hidden behind iron masks
Only to please themselves.

The love of money, and not to love
Their neighbors as themselves
Is their pride.
Devoid of compassion,
Resisting love,
Apathy is their bliss.

Friendship

Red, yellow, green balloons.
Kicking them,
Throwing them.
Look! It touched my nose.
Cuddly, squishy, "skweshy",
Then I let it go.

What fun to play with a friend.
The smell of cookies out of the oven.
Yum! It melts into my mouth.
My little friend has
Chocolate all over her mouth.
She beat me to it— this time
To scrape and lick out the bowl.
She laughs and takes one more bite.

Sharing stories with my friends.
Hugs and kisses
Dressing up in cool clothes
Going out,
Seeing places and new faces,
Artworks or the zoo.

It's wonderful being with friends that I know
Sharing secrets,
Frustrations too.

I'd love to kick a "footie"
But I can't.
With friends around me
For a chat and a laugh,
It's fine to watch
And cheer them on.

A kind word
A gentle touch,
Just showing me that I am cared for,
Wanted and loved
Makes life worthwhile and fun.

I'd love to climb a mountain
Maybe a tree as well
Or just run along a beach
And feel the sand between my toes.

But most of all
My friends are like the precious jewels
That sparkle in a princess crown.
Or, like the stars
That twinkle in the night,
The moon without her rays
Just cannot be.
That's how my friends,
Young and old
Are so special to me.

I may not dance
But I can fly a kite
That soars up high into the sky
On winds unseen,
Like my dreams.
I do have some.

Adventures – I have them in my mind.
Let me never be
Without a hug, a warm embrace,
The caring, sharing love of a friend.

Heaven Bound

In the will of God
I am at peace.
The Holy Spirit can move freely from God to me, and me to God.
Life is like walking through daisies.
Soft underneath to the touch of my feet.
Crumpled but not crushed.
Gentle breezes blow through my hair,
And the waft of intoxicating perfumes of roses
Filling me with a sense of freedom.

Freedom that I am in God and Christ is in me.
Freedom that I belong to the Great "I AM."
God, My Father, My Friend, My Savior.

When I am in His will
I can let the sun caress and kiss me.
When the dew drops fall
He'll soak them up again.

When disaster and despair comes my way
Swifter than an arrow's mark
You shield me from all trouble and foes.
I will not need to run or fear.

I will call your name.
If I fall in trembling, frail humanity
You will pick me up.

Put me high upon an eagle's wings
And I'll soar above these trials.
No harm can come to me.

One day you will lift me,
Embracing me into your kingdom,
To live with You forever. Eternity

The Tree

The Tree

Oh tree of rapture and of dignity
You hold me fast
Embracing me.

In your warm bosom
I lay sheltered.
Protected from the harshness of this life,
The ugliness,
Devouring,
Cruelties that surround me.

Here I lay
Contented,
Knowing that whatever happens
I am in safe haven.

Always a child,
I am obedient to you
Lord Jesus Christ.

I cry for you to help me always.
Before I am laid in my silent grave.
Help me Lord
As tears fall
Hot upon my face.
This world is harsh.
I fear I'll fall.

Cruelty and harshness
Provokes in me an anger.
I turn to you
For constant help.

God, as you nourish the tree
In this unforgiving land
I am held close to your breast,
Secure.

The Ballet Class

When I watch the ballet class
My soul rests.
I am transported to a place of peace and love.
With each pirouette my heart skips a beat.
I gasp for air at this beauteous sight.
The maestro with eagle eyes,
Watching, correcting with care
Each placement, each life-giving breath.

I am in awe to see such a beautiful creation at work.
The mind so fervent to perfect each step.
Dance with abandonment of soul
Through storms and sunny days.
To show a part of God's great handiwork to us.
The strength and gentleness we contain
Like trees standing strong.
Leaves, delicate, rustling in the breezes.

So the dance rehearsal now has ended
And I am left a better person
For having shared in this wonderful gift
Of life and love,
This dedication.

Childhood

As a child I laughed, and danced and sang.
Sweet melodies and talk flowed from my mouth
Out of a happy, thankful heart.
Happy that I was alive
To breathe the soft air,
Fragrances of perfumes
From forest trees.
To touch the snow
And feel caressed.

White blanket covering me
As I rolled down the hill.
The smell of cookies grandma made
Told me I was loved, needed,
Enfolded by security.
The warmth from hearths, hugs and laughter.
Listening to, and answering, all my many questions of
The whys and wherefores.
My mind always delving, always curious, always challenging.

Perfumes of forest flowers
Showed me so much joy was here in life.
To take, to use, and to enjoy.
A never-ending stream of adventures lay
A golden path tread.

Surrounded by goodness.
I also saw not all were loving, kind,
These were to be avoided.

Yet I was blessed.
For as a child I was protected from fierce winds.
Of cruel-doing souls.

I know the laughter of friendships and acceptance
And the freedom to express the soul in me.
Of dancing Ring-a-Rosie
And other playful games.

Being treated with dignity
And learning to respect
Those that I meet.

My heart was young
I knew God's love.
I yearned for love like this
To last forever.

The Bird Set Free

On the wings of a dove
I've been set free
The Holy Spirit at last
Takes flight in me.
The movement of love
Is too much to contain.
He moves in, then out, through me.
The movement freely touching others.
What peace I have
To know joy like this
Can rest with me in some other soul.
I am His vessel
Such privilege
Such joy.

As he teaches me
More of God's love for me and you.
Love pours into my soul.
I'm filled with ecstasy
To know I'm alive.
He belongs in me.
My heart pulse belonging to Him.

He is set free, this bird in me.
At last, contained no more.
I can move in truth with Him

So touch the lives of others
Through this vessel, me.

Then the world may see
That Jesus Christ is living
And broken hearts be healed.
Lives are changed
God and Kingdom glorified.

Just 'cause, one let
The bird go free.
'Cause at last the bird in me is free.

Lyn

When you first met Lyn, she was uncomely to look at. Rather dull in her conversation. No big dreams. No big goals. Her appearance certainly did not greet you as a beauteous or even interesting form.

She was very ordinary yet this plain person drew me to want to know her. She had a distinct air of simplicity about her. Her surroundings betrayed a woman who was content in her position as a wife and a mother of four, fast growing, and demanding children.

These children had a wonderful environment— nurtured, allowed to express and be themselves. No great demands were placed on them. They were loved, accepted and could just be.

I sensed a bond, a unity, a caring for each other in that home.

Yet it had none of the glamour of the "average" family. No modern trappings or conveniences pervaded that family. Ordinary, though not without their personal struggles.

Lyn came from a background of stability. She met and, after two years, married Alfredo after two years' courtship. They married, not out of necessity, convenience, nor for status. They were not pressured by family members. They married because they were blissfully in love.

I later discovered that Lyn does have a dream. She never received an education. Not because she could not cope. Lyn was secretly doing courses to improve herself. I then began to see in her some inner strengths.

To be so ordinary, to be there for her children, to enjoy her husband even now, and be happy with her lot, with its ups and downs, is something I admire. This ordinariness is what I strive for.

Lyn is accepted, and is comfortable with herself.

A mighty gift she has. I would not trade her life for all the jewels that can be had. She is a priceless gem, herself. Her husband sees and appreciates her as she is. Lyn is one who'll leave a positive mark on this earth. Her children revel in her love, her being. That's gold. They'll always know their mother is there for them.

I think how much more they have than all who have material splendors. I find peace and rest in her family. The children belong— no fancy stuff, no airs or graces and no hypocrisy, no being what you're not.

More people can learn from Lyn to be just who they are. Imperfect, yet acceptable. When I see Lyn, I can be myself. I don't need intellectual conversations. I can be as quiet or outgoing as I please.

To me Lyn is extraordinarily beautiful. I like her simple, happy personality. She doesn't need to be an intellect, or walk with haughty gait.

Lyn doesn't wear the latest fashions. Nor is her home decorated with expensive furnishings.

She has won my admiration. I like her as she is.

Her beauty is in her being just the way she is.

"Come inside, Lyn. Sit down and have a 'cuppa'."

Sophia

An impish face, yet not without compassion, lay cradling large, warm, animated eyes. There was an air of determination. I thought her haughty at first impression. I found she was gentle yet ready at all times to defend herself and her achievements.

Sophia came from Italian background. Strict discipline did not suit her. She reveled at times to rebel. Quick to defend her beliefs and actions yet willing to listen to others.

This fiery, independent woman had a childhood that had drained her of her joy in being herself. She always had to live up to the expectations and approval from her parents. They were, like so many parents, unable to accept her for the beauty that she was. They couldn't accept and praise her for her worth. When something was not quite right, her parents were focused on her faults.

Sophia wanted so much to be free of her rigid, formal upbringing.

She fought not to be someone's clone or puppet. Sophia longed to dance, to grow, to laugh in soft breezes. To listen to whispers of love. To be drenched in the excitement of love and freedom.

As a teenager, Sophia did moderately well at school, with all the dreams and aspirations of any young woman. She had goals of love, and of having her own identity. She dreamt of a solitary life in a faraway place, perhaps on a mountaintop, where she could laugh and be accepted as herself.

Sophia had a brain, and her own personal charm. She left school early and got her first job at age 16 in the local supermarket.

Married at 18, Sophia had three children. Disillusionment crept in and led to divorce. Forced back to work, she was shrewd. She saved her money, eventually buying a house, while still providing for her children. Sophia still had dreams that she hoped, one day, would be fulfilled.

Life took a happy turn for Sophia when she stepped out to socially engage and contribute to her community. Sophia discovered she was well liked and even popular, through her tennis club activities. Sophia also took a sewing class and found enjoyment and worthiness in making clothes for herself, her children and for others.

Though life at times was difficult, this resilient woman proved her strength. She could not be defeated. People admired her. Her personality attracted nurturing people into her life. Even when she felt defeated, she would not yield to this destructive master.

In strength she grew, and won the approval of her children.

She learned through life to accept herself, to be confident and free.

Lady and her Dog

A woman took a walk. It was still sunny, though at times the sun would disappear behind a cloud and the breeze would chill the body.

She enjoyed taking her dog for a walk, breathing in fresh air, enjoying the many different shapes and colors of old buildings. They seemed so individual, just like the people in them — alike, yet leading different lives. They each had a different character. Perhaps their likes, dislikes and personalities were etched on the building themselves.

There was a gentle breeze. In the distance were the hills sunbathing in golden streams, irregular sprawling shapes that one could almost touch. At times she sensed such oneness with them, with all of nature. It seemed to her that if she could breathe in deeply enough, she could snuggle in amongst it all. How she longed to do just that.

The parklands seemed very spacious. Barely a soul was there.

A mother patiently tended to her little child. Squeals of delight could be heard each time the swing went up. The mother was content in her child's pure joy.

She enjoyed the open spaces and freedom. Flowers and roses boarded the pathways, like an oil painting dotted with bright, red, pink and yellow hues. The autumn leaves showed off the soft, warm, orange tones, leaving the landscape broken. It was as if the earth was showing off.

"Here am I, so beautiful, graceful and tender."

The woman observed rich delights in her surroundings that gave pleasure to her soul. Yet, most would not see this. How downhearted the earth must feel to have her beauty overlooked? Worse, the lady observed that rubbish was strewn around a park bench. The bench itself had been smashed to pieces. The earth must cry out. So too, this lady's heart cried out in affinity with the land. There was sweetness in their shared sorrow. She reached down and stroked her dog, and he nudged close to her.

This elegant woman had gone unnoticed, unappreciated, unloved, and had in times past been stolen from, left with nothing but pain and scars. She could identify with the scars left on nature's path, scars caused by people. She too, had been betrayed so often, her beauty often crushed.

As the smell of a rose filled her senses, she could still believe and dream. There was hope that goodness still remained, that beauty still lived, made stronger through despair and destruction. It flourished, blossomed, smiling, forgiving and strong.

The woman looked around her as her dog stopped to sniff under a tree. Birds flew and chirping noisily. The dog romped and played, barking with joyful abandonment.

She noticed there was a man in the distance, with a dog larger than hers. Her own little pet ran to greet the other dog. Both animals began to play, happy and oblivious to all the cares around them.

The lady and the stranger introduced themselves and began to talk. Mainly she talked and he listened. He listened so well, that she went on and on, like a tightly wound up spring, suddenly released.

The lady felt free. Free to air her opinions, and when someone really listened to her she found it hard to stop.

They started with small talk and local gossip. They went on to share their disillusionment and frustrations about the injustices of the world in which they lived.

They looked at their dogs having fun together.

Though the man wasn't particularly handsome, and was of small stature, she found him to have a gentle, caring nature. As he stood still, he looked at her and said, "Would you like to come out for dinner tomorrow night?"

Their eyes met. She smiled, and took in a deep breath, consumed with joy. With a twinkle in her eyes, she said "Yes!"

The Basket

Cool waters
Gliding
Catching golden sparkles from the midday sun.
Waves gently lapping at the sides of the basket.
Made by God's Hands
To keep us safe and warm.
Letting go
Into God's Hands.
Trusting in Him…
Is there any other option?
Nowhere do we travel
But by God's direction.

I have let go.
Trusting where He leads us.
While around us is
Fighting, strife, raging storms of malice.
Revenge, selfishness,
Hardened hearts.
Self-striving, fears, anxieties, unkindness.

We move gracefully on the velvet waters
Shielded by His Love.
The only touch is the occasional brush of tall grasses
Upon our cheeks,
As a mother's touch of
Needing,

Being wanted and loved.
Knowing that He keeps us safe,
Controlling every moment of our lives.
He knows.
He is working for all our good
For His Glory.

You and I are in this basket
Woven so lovingly to keep us dry.
So, we rest in His Arms.
I don't know where He leads us
What His plans for us are (completely).
I know only He knows what is best.
We are under His everlasting, ever-giving arms
I trust in Him.

Just like Moses in the basket.
A vulnerable situation…
Trusting in God,
His mother put him in.
Believing in Hope,
That Moses would be kept safe.

Out of this terrible position
Moses was not only kept safe
But God's Hand gave him the best of care
And raised Him for His Glory
To perform mighty works for Him.

Beloved

Cover me, Oh Lord
That I may always seek and find You
As you sought and found me.

To be embraced by You
And to know You as You know me
Is rest and peace.

So I can go on in hope with Thee.
Knowing I belong to love.
What peace
What joy
What confidence I have
In safe
Caring love I live.

Words find it hard to express this meaning.
As in a mother's womb I lay.
Safe,
Protected,
From all harm's way,
Cradled, fed and nurtured.

So precious,
So priceless,
Just as I lay in comfort.
I am loved.

In all the plans made for me
Only the best shall be given.

And me, a mum, with a happy heart that leaps
With thoughts for my unborn babe
For what is good.
Will this fit or that?
Will this go with that?
This baby is just the most precious soul.
I love her as she is.
One day in my arms she'll rest
And I'll delight in loving her.

With growth comes discipline
Though painful it must be
To set you right
Upon God's path.
To know and do His Will.
For that is victory in life.
A life of love and peace
Where joys will never cease.

I sit here,
Amazed.
That God loves me so much.
He gave His life, His all for me.
He wants to have fellowship with me
And I with Him.

I seek him.
I want to know him,
To do His will.
Walking,
Ever trusting
In His love so pure.
Knowing with my Savior
I am secure.

God Lives

My heart rejoices in the Living God
For what he's done for me
What he does and continues to do for me
And for my family.
My heart bursts forth in gratitude.
His care and His forgiveness sets me free.
To do His will, to worship Him,
Obey His word.

Though life in Christ is not an easy path,
It is the *only* path to tread.
With the sorrows, intense griefs, trials,
Rejections and pain,
The lonely times with heartaches to complete.

My life is filled with His peace, ecstatic joy and love,
Compelling me to yearn more and more
That flesh in me be dead.
So none of me
And *all* of Christ
Can dwell,
Possess the very breath I take.

The "my" is no more,
Only Christ's life
Is.
This is my hope.

To give him all the glory that is His.
The self in me is dead.

The wonder of this unity with Him.
Now abundant,
Happy life,
And for eternity with Jesus Christ,
The living God, my Savior,
My best friend.

Song

How can I thank God?
What gratitude can I express?
That He has given me such a gift
The gift of Love?
The Holy Spirit
Indwelling and flowing out of me,
What comfort I receive
Enfolded in His arms.

What a privilege I have
To have the great I AM.
The Alpha and the Omega,
Creator of the Universe
Alive,
Living in and through me.

Oh may I, with rejoicing heart
Allow His love
That He, with sacrifice
Has given to me.
To share with others
In brotherly love
This jewel.

Help me Lord to not hold onto it
For self.
For then I know I lose the precious
Perfume of Your sweet love.
In giving I gain
To receive some more.

Help me never to forget
That in dying to self
And giving Your love to others
You live.

Expressive Poem

He is not in some far-off distant galaxy.
He is walking, living, breathing with me
And He dwells in me.

What a marvel
What a joy
To know that My Savior
Is a Person
With all the emotions and feelings that I have,
Far deeper than anyone could understand.

He is a Person,
  Without sin.

Yet He gave His life for me
Took upon Himself my filthiness
And clothed me in His righteousness.

Such a person could never be
With such great love for me.
He picked me up and took my place.
Set me way on high
With all the riches and blessings and safety
That I could never find.

He put Himself in hell for me
Set me free.
Such love I never can
Nor will I ever comprehend.

Worry

Beginning like a tiny, burning ember
Stealthily creeping,
Deceptive,
Hidden.
Like growing roots,
Digging, breathing, grasping
Into the very sinews of the soul.

The damage that it does
Suffocating the soul that cries in pain.
The flame of fear grows stronger
Embracing in its crippling path
Anxiety.

Where flames of terror
Strike with open force
To stab the heart
Pain increases with self-desire.
To strive for answers
Doing my will
Just increases the intensity of the
Flames of Worry.

Jesus comes to me and says,
  "My little child,
Are you not beloved of God?
  Did I not die for you?

Forgive you of your sins?
Come rest in me,
And give all your burdens to me.

Did I not carry you when you were down,
Ill, broken and discarded?
Why do you continue to doubt?
I am the Alpha and the Omega.
I made the heavens and the earth
And I am your best friend.
You know, and yet continue to doubt in
My love and care for you.
You worry because you will not stop to listen to my voice.
Headstrong you run, and lean upon your own understanding;
Rather than letting go, accepting, praising and
Thanking me for everything."

The Son of God continued,
"Not thy will but My will be done.
So it is written in My word.
You continue to resist,
To 'wait on Me.'

You run on worry and fear
Getting anxious,
Allowing the fire of destruction to burn you out.
For what purpose?
Is that My will for you on this earth?

I've come to give you life abundant,
Now and for Eternity!

Yet for how long will you continue to resist my love for you?
Free, never-ending, ever-giving.
I tell you, 'rest in Me, wait on Me, trust in Me.'
I have made all good for you.

Don't let worry be your entertainment.
Pray to Me and praise Me continually.
Obey my Word.

Know that you have the power over all of the power
Of the enemy.
The evil one cannot touch you.
I have covered you with
My blood.
Claim this power
I have given you.

You are strengthened, loved and protected!
You can rest alongside the banks of cool waters.
Soak up the glistening sun.
Receive My love for you,
So live whole and healed!"

Through the fires of woes and sins,
The little shoots of green life in me sprout upwards, heavenwards.
I return to rest in you.
To be loved, protected, and with your faith in me grown stronger
Through the scars.
Once again I trust in You my Lord.
My Love for you."

*S*tage Debut

When I married my husband, I was blessed to inherit his two beautiful boys and young daughter. We later on had two more children. I regarded them all as my own.

One of my little boys played in the concert last night, the concert with many young children playing in bands – of clarinets, trumpets and a big, bass drum.

The violins were played sweetly, with nervous, little hands. The concentration of the children encouraged me that life goes on with beauty still around.

The little voices of the choir made our hearts glad. We cheered with joy.

Our little boy played in the concert last night. With great anticipation, we waited for his turn. He would not look or smile at us at first. So serious was this fun! We waved to him. He waved back. Then he made a "shshshsh" sound, with his finger to his mouth. He shyly hid his pride.

He looked so smart in his white shirt, black pants and shoes.

Then songs were sung. Lovely melodies were made. The teachers showed great care in ensuring all the students did their best.

We could see God's love shown in that.

Next, our boy, with all the others, took a recorder to his mouth.

He played. Like listening to accomplished musicians, that's how proud we felt this night. Yes, our little boy played in the concert last night.

We remember when he first began.

"Mum, we're learning the recorder today."

There was only three dollars to pay. We bought one with excitement, no less for our boy. He began with notes that whistled and screeched.

He persevered.

We encouraged him to keep on going, though at times he felt like quitting. Then one day came the dreaded moment,

"Mum and Dad, I want to give it up. I don't want to play anymore. I can't get it. I hate the recorder."

We encouraged him not to stop. "It's beautiful. Keep going. We enjoy your playing very much."

I prayed to God he would not stop. I even liked the wrong, clumsy notes. He's playing music. He's so beautiful and strong. He can do it. I know he can.

The three minute practices initially were such an ordeal, requiring coaxing and encouragement.

Suddenly, one day we heard such sweet music coming from our son's room. Could that be our boy? The notes came out so clear, like a bird's song happily coming forth, enjoying its very being.

There we found him, happy on his bed, playing little songs and melodies. Twenty minutes passed.

I asked his father, "Did you encourage him to practice?"

"No. He did it on his own."

Our hearts were filled with gratitude. He practiced on his own. We thanked the Lord. It is evident a little encouragement can go a long way.

At the end of the concert, our son asked us with great eagerness, "can I see the violin teacher?" We introduced him to the strings instructor. He was given a warm welcome.

"Hello" said the teacher, "so you want to play the violin?"

"Yes", replied a little voice.

We were ready for the scrapes and scratches of his initial notes. I wondered with excitement, what melodies he would learn to play, as lots of practice and joys lay ahead for him.

Our little boy played in the concert last night.

A Simple Man

I met a man called Bob.
A man who was passed over.
Nobody saw the beauty he could offer.
He was a simple man,
An unassuming man.
A man of no financial wealth,
His clothes are not fine raiment.
Silk, he will never wear.

Yet, he has lived for many years on dry, parched, brown land.
He has witnessed drought and floods.
Bob has done things many would not dare to do.
This simple man loves the land and has nurtured it with respect.
He has trod and rode on this ground through hardship and distress.
He found that being honest offers man his rest.

Bob's riding days are over but his character is not lost.
We can learn from men such as these.
True values are the best.
Money does not bring happiness and peace of heart.

He was a simple man
Not schooled in high class
Yet I have learned from him
That God loves the humble heart.

Sunset

Delicate lacework.
Lean trunks silhouetted against a soft
Orange-salmon and pale blue sky.
Like a pretty, dotted pastel-colored tapestry.
Deep green, grey dots and dark streaks of branches across the sky.
Getting deeper,
The washes of orange intensify
As the eye wanders across this palette.
The dots so intricately woven
Are complex in design
The lines become bolder and thicker.
More brilliant, the wash becomes.

This handiwork of God is not only a glorious picture.
It is a haven for birds, giving food and shelter.
A striking scene, a changing one.
It never stays the same.

Yet God's love touches me that same night.
I marvel at the wondrous love he has for me,
In stretching out his arms,
Welcoming me,
Home.
Such tenderness I feel in His security.
To know I'm loved by Him.
I'm cared for by Him, who created this earth and heaven too.

To know I'm cared for by such a God
Is beauty on its own.

The wash is deepening now,
Sky merging with trees.
Dots are disappearing into the black expanse.

Sunset.

His love
His care
Is here forever.

Log

Log

The log across the rocks is
Suspended,
Motionless.
Waves are crashing below.
I wish this moment could never stop.
So beautiful it is.
Strength and peace abound
Like a warm embrace.
It is the forever,
Yet soon it will be gone.
This moment is captured,
As if in space.

This log is looking on,
A never ending witness.
This place is real,
The beauty here.
These rocks have seen many washes.
Her tender strokes, her harsh rebukes
Can my time stand still?
Does this have to end for me?

My heart says, "Stop!"
"Slow down,"
I am glad that I obey.
I'll take these moments, and all my dreams,
Back home with me today.

I'll face the trials of ordinary living
And of the blows my foes hand out.
I'll face them better now.
I have seen the majesty of the Lord.
Felt his presence and
Sat in the stillness and wonder of His creation.
I breathe in His love and strength,
Sit still
Among this beauty.
I know that He is with me.
This will never stop.
It is unending.

Memories of My Husband

Frangipani petals floating down the stream
Cool bubbling water
Tumbling over smooth rocks
Oozing out the sweet pungent perfumes of pink frangipani.
Magnolia bushes edge the stream.
Memories of you and me
Laughing.
Lying in a soft carpet of dew covered grasses.
Inhaling.
Covering us like a patchwork blanket.
We love as our skins fuse with one another.
Resting.
Allowing the sun's rays softened by dancing leaves
Against the sun
To renew our strength.
Infusing us with the Creator's love and life.

I feel like living.
I want to live.
So sings my being,
As I breathe in these fragrances.
Sweet and powerful.
Compelling me to live.
To give of God's love
To everyone I come across.

I see His beauty everywhere.
I feel His presence.
I inhale the smell of hope.
I run and dance.
The forest is my benefactor.
The whole earth is my protector.
The hills, the valleys, embrace me
As a mother suckles her young.
Even the needles of the pine trees
Prick me with His love.
Just to breathe in one breath,
God's freshness,
Is pure joy.

Ice Dance

Gliding,
Free,
Bird-like,
Majestic.
As my skates fly across this frozen lake,
On hardened ice beneath my feet,
I am as free as an eagle that soars above the cliffs.
Then in the nest,
Secure.
I sit still to rest.
Dance in joyous rhythms of contentment.
Movements rare and pure.
Blades shimmer.
This dance is intense with passionate ecstasy.

Then, confident in quiet security
Protected in God's embrace,
Exhilaration fills my soul,
Knowing that I am known.
Cared for by the Living God
At home in His Love.

As the mother eagle feeds her chicks
With open mouths
I receive the banquet prepared by God.

Adventure on the ice,
Amazement at every turn and leap!
A knowledge and growth that never ends.
Delight and peace fills my soul
At this journey's end.

Meaning

I am so alone,
Grief choked within my breast.
Yet I can see
This is how it's meant to be.
Teaching me to be still
And rest in Thee.

Trusting in the Lord
While rivers of tears
Etch my cheeks.
My eyes burn.
I learn to rest and not to strive,
Accept.

I see the leaves upon the trees,
Feel the gentle breeze upon my skin.
The perfume of flowers
Invades my senses
Awakening beauty.

With gratitude I know
I am loved by God,
Who gave His life
For you and me,
Freed us from sin;
Who created Heaven and Earth
And all that dwells therein

My soul enriched
As I ponder on this truth.
With peace I write this poem.
Joy floods my being.
I think upon the painting I am about to begin.

Yellow Flowers

What is the purpose of living?
What is it all about?
If not to live for Him.
If not to do,
If not to be,
For Him.

I see the bright yellow flower
His peace is here
I see the strength, beauty and freedom
He has for me.
All I must do is reach out
And pluck it.

He warms me
As the sun coats the petals
  With rays of growth.
He caresses me
  With a breeze of hope.
I look beyond
And see the yellow carpet
  Spread out before me.
I want to walk on top of it.

As I crush the petals beneath my bare feet,
A sweet scent invades my nostrils,
I am as vulnerable as those flowers.

I once believed in the goodness of life.
Like the petals beneath me
I have been broken.

Yet through the brokenness
Christ will make me His vessel.
Like the broken flowers
His divine perfume will flow out of me.
Blue skies above white clouds.
I see the reason for living—
For Him,
For the Lord Jesus Christ!

Not Insignificant

As I sit in awe,
In Your presence,
Lord,
I look at a blade of grass.

I marvel at the tiny veins
And see the lovely greens.
Each blade is slightly different
In shape than another.
There are millions of blades.

"Many O Lord are thy wonderful works
Which thou hast done?"
I see the leaves on the trees around me.
Each leaf is slightly different in shape.
Flowers, birds, the soil, sun, sky, clouds.

How could anyone disbelieve your very existence?

You who made all these marvelous beauties to enjoy
Are the same resurrected Christ,
The living God,
Who came to us,
Brought us the Good News,
Was crucified,
Resurrected,
Then left us your power by the Holy Spirit.

You are God,
You are life,
You are love.

Acceptance

As the moss growing on the rock
Is accepted by the lapping waters,
Exposing vivid greens.

As the spider accepts the offering from the web it weaves
To watch and eat its prey.

As the ground accepts the stem
That holds the golden flower above,
And the sun and moon accept the earth

So I too bask in the delight
Of being accepted
By the God who created earth and all that is held in it.

The joy, the bliss,
To be accepted,
To just be.
No expectations.
Teaching me to put none on others.
To be.

It is wonderful to know I am loved,
Held in esteem,
Respected.
Made worthy
As I am.

To be with love
In love,
So I can run and dance
In freedom.
Forgiven.
I can find myself
As I have been found.

Threshold

I may not know how to love perfectly.
Mistakes,
I've made so many.
At times my heart has hardened like a stone.
Until I realise, I have so much.
In His love I bask.

A guarantee of treasures
Way beyond what my mind
Can comprehend.
He gives, and gives,
And gives to me,
Mercies,
Patience,
Forgiveness.
Like stones worn by water and sand
I absorb and receive Your enduring kindness.

Those sharp rocks that lead my path to life,
Still pierce my feet with sore challenges.
I still must learn.

In all of this,
I am loved,
Carried
By my Abba Father
To Eternity.
Perfected by His grace.

Regret

My husband was a very special man.
 With great laughter and humor
His smile would light up the world
And joy would flood my soul.
His positive attitude
 Lifted me above the dross.
All fear was dispelled.

He celebrated life.
 The strength of God's love
Flowed through him,
Encouraging me
With passionate love.

It's just so rare
To find a man like him,
Yet I often took him for granted.
I didn't, at times, appreciate him
Or what I had with him.

Now he's gone.
Alone, I live with some regrets.
But I am so grateful for my memories
Of happy times with him.

I know what real love is.
If I could bring him back,

This is what I would say,
"Thank you for all the love.
You were the good in my life.
You sacrificed everything for my healing and happiness."

I have experienced great love
Irreplaceable.
Eternal.

Freed by Love

He talks to me in breezes
Soft, gentle, cooling wafts of wind
Gently knock on my mind.
Refreshing,
Touching me tenderly
Reminding me of you.

Running through bushes
Streams flowing by
Bubbling with stones of mischief,
Of life,
Of fun.

I lie awake,
Dreaming,
Of frangipani and magnolia perfumes.
Memories of love shared.

Sadness and joys
Tears and laughter.
I remember you told me
How beautiful I was.
You touched my face
With one soft brush of your finger.
Warmth poured into my soul,
Filling my every fiber with God's love.

Strength saturated me.
I could do anything I wanted to.
I was filled and satisfied
With the beauty of the sunshine.

And I loved.
I gave myself to you and God.
I saw the beauty in a leaf
And marveled at tree trunks.
I felt the goodness of just being.

I was wrapped in a silken garment.
I breathed in the freshness of
Mountaintops.

I was the one amongst the loveliest of flowers,
A garland picked.
Chosen, at one with many beauties:
Daisies, pine trees, grasses, wild flowers, leaves.
So special.
Alone, yet surrounded by infinite love.

Resting Place

O come sweet Jesus,
Take my hand.
What divine harmony it is
To be with You.

Treading lightly with sweet angels.
I kiss your fingers.
Soft, I depart.

See my crumpled, weary body
The one marked by defeat.
My spirit leaves this human lump of dust,
Runs and clings to you.

With Your freedom that You give
I glide eternally with You.
I go where flowers never lose perfume.
I stand right by a twinkling star.
There's so much adventure,
So much fun.
Surrounded by Your great love
Enfolded by mystery.

Such rapture can't be described
I am one and You are one with me.
What treasure I behold.

A whisper cannot convey the splendor of Your love.
Knowing You as You know me.

In God's arms
I'm finally at rest and so secure,
With Him always.
Praises echo from my soul
My happiness sings to what you've brought me through.
I bask in your light
Your ever-giving love.
I rest in your great arms
My head upon You.
And just "be."

I am loved forever, eternally.
Now I know You freely,
Face to face.
In my small, simple way
I know You love me.
Worshipping You
Is bliss.

Vessel

Come Holy Spirit
Possess me, all of me.

In my frailties make me grow.
Strengthen me to do God's will,
That the gospel of the Lord
Might, to all I meet and see, be given.

I pray that the word I speak is truth.
That the deeds I do are flowing from His love.
Your love You freely gave to me.

May I speak proclaiming of Your love to broken people,
To the disillusioned and troubled?
I pray I can lead them to Your Presence.

Please allow the Holy Spirit to work through me
To share God's love with others.

I pray that I may not be a stumbling block
Of doubts, judgments and my own insecurities.
That, as I look to You,
Your love flows out as I share the Gospel message.

Lady with Huge Flowered Hat

I saw her on the footpath in Ryde. Bags were tied to her wheelchair. People passed her by. Some chuckled but tried to hide the funny side.

I was drawn to speak, wanting to know her. She sat, contented, as though ready for entry on a stage where hundreds would applaud.

I looked into her face. She was in fact, pretty but masked by heavy make-up. There she sat, a painting of serenity splashed in joyous colors, about 70 years old.

"Hello. Your hat is so beautiful and the flowers are so colorful," I remarked."

"Thank you love, so glad you like them. I've spent the last three months making them myself from scraps I find. People also give me fabric pieces from time to time. I've got a bit of arthritis but I still manage to put the flowers onto the hat. You love my hat?"

"Yes!" I exclaimed, smiling.

She went on, "The brim is wide and protects my skin from the sun. Not that it's young anymore."

I offered to help take her wheelchair into the shop.

She politely declined, "I come here and stay a while most days. People hurry by for coffee and a newspaper. They're in such a rush but I enjoy watching them. Occasionally someone nice like you stops and chats a while. Makes my day, love."

I continued, "You have a lovely face and smile."

She said wistfully, "I still like to make myself look as beautiful as I can. I like the make-up. Why not smile? Life still has a lot of good in it."

I pointed to a flower. "I really love that pink rose."

She replied, "Thank you, love. I like the bright red and purple ones." Excitedly she continued, "And see the little orange ones? They are fiddly to stick in. The old arthritis."

Proudly she said, "I do all the cutting and wiring by myself. Glad you like the show."

Looking into the distance my new friend said, "Tom brought me flowers. Never missed a week. We lived in a little house in Surry Hills. Them were the days. I wear the flowers in my hat, 'cos then it is like Tom is with me now. Married for forty years, we were. No-one knows the sadness in my heart now he's gone. My best mate was Tom. None kinder or truer you could find."

She paused, lost in the past, "He'd always stroke my hand when trouble came and say, 'She'll be okay.' He'd then make the best 'cuppa' you can drink."

The lady talked on, "I remember when he took me to my first stage show. We laughed. Loved every bit of it. He's gone now. Ten years. I miss him, love. Gee but it's good to talk to you. I haven't talked like this to anyone in a long while."

With a twinkle in her eyes she explained, "He was a 'postie' back in those days, fit and handsome. He looked great in uniform. We met at a local dance. He wouldn't stop looking at me, nor I him. And oh, the girls, they all had an eye for him. Women would sit at the gate and get their mail from him by hand. But me, I knew he loved me most of all. He was mine."

The elderly woman continued with pride, "Tom once did such an act of bravery. He ran into the waves at Bondi. Three children got into great trouble. A rip had got them. Tom, not thinking of himself, rushed in 'boots and all.' He was nearly swept away. He could have drowned. He lay exhausted, the little ones beside him on the sand, until some people came to help. He saved those three. Tom often told me I wonder how they're doing now. I reckon he'd have loved to see them one more time. That's the kind of bloke he was. I miss him heaps."

I finally got a word in, "Are you enjoying your life?"

"My life's good," she said.

She went on, "Soon I'll be wandering down the street. See my bag? There's bread and fish in there. Takes me about ten minutes to get to the park. They're always waiting for me. They're hungry now. My friends. They like my hat, alright, as well. You should see them, landing on my hat and even taking from my hand! I feed them every day. I must, otherwise they'll go hungry. That just will not do."

The lady continued, "Then I drive home. Floss, our cat, greets me.

Tom brought her home twelve years ago. A tiny bundle, like an orange cotton reel. Gets lonely sometimes without my Tom. Floss knows I've come home even before the key reaches the lock. She rubs herself against my legs, then jumps onto my lap. So glad you stopped to chat with me. You've made me happy. Well I'd better be off to feed my family. They're all expecting me. And what did you say? You've got to get back to work? Well, have a lovely day."

I said goodbye, the usual, "Nice to have met you," but I really meant it. As I walked away, I felt my life had been enriched by meeting such a soul as Elsie. She was happy and led a simple life. There was a richness there. I thought, "Yes, I hope one day I'll have a man like Tom".

I wanted to be as good a wife as Elsie.

I saw in one brief moment that the sweetest essence of life comes from caring for and being loved in return. Hope within my soul was once more renewed.

Sometimes I wonder how Elsie is getting on.

A Bush Scene

Strong shoes for walking are put on.
Silence.
Only the smells of wild bush trees.
Insects break the crisp, dry air
with spiders who dare to spread their webs,
join in a symphony of sounds.
A lullaby.
A bird or two fly into the tree leaves,
adding notes to enhance the bush choir.
On this dirt path we walk,
crunching the dry, brown, green leaves beneath our feet.
There is not a living soul here – just you and me.
Excited by this little journey,
that we know will lead us into a new adventure.

We stop, look with joy into one another's eyes,
hug – warm, contentment,
confident in our love for one another.
Stopping a while, we share this happy moment.
Then kiss with satisfied gratitude, that we have come this far.
Our feet march on in session,
to the praying leaves and singing insects.
Contentment enfolds us both with tender care.

Far off we see rocks and stones.
The ground is split.

Dry, hard clay.
We still are alone, only the sound of a little wind.

Then before our eyes,
a display of quiet country setting.
Blue cloudless skies oversee fields of lush green grasses dotted
amongst
a vast landscape of red and brown tones; as if we were stepping
into a master painting.
Trees are few, yet large.
Not a soul in sight.
This is all in view.
As we walk, we see a wire fence.
With cheeky joy we venture inside,
to explore, and to run
in this wonderful canvassed panorama.
We are here by invitation,
to partake of its freedom and beauty.
This land that feeds the hungry souls,
nourishing each fibre of every being,
and beats within our hearts.
Like a newborn child, warm rays creep through with golden wash.

We are glad to be alive, free and strong.
Standing lazily, our legs give way to our desire to lie down on the
soft grass.
Feeling confident, we revelled in the silence and watched the sky
cover us with peace.
We chattered only a little, and drew in with each breath, the magic
of this unspoken beauty.

Suddenly, from out of nowhere, we saw the bulls staring down
at us.
No longer oblivious to the danger here,
we both sat up amazed, and then terrified!

Slowly, we stood up and began to pray "Dear God - help us!"
We were in grave danger.

About twenty, horned beasts surrounded us,
circled us, standing proud.
We were their target, unknown to us
and bewildered at this sight.
They began to move towards us.
Solid horns protruded from huge forms.
To this day I am still amazed that we did not panic.
Momentarily afraid we stood, we prayed even harder for Divine
intervention.
Two or more of these beasts began to dig the earth with their
hooves, shaking their heads, snorting at us. It was terrifying as
they made the circle smaller.

Suddenly, I remembered that a while ago, I saw a film with
Vanessa Redgrave being at a picnic in a similar setting; where
a gang of bulls began to charge at her. Her immediate reaction
was to run towards the steers, screaming and yelling with arms
opened wide. To my amazement the animals were frightened off
by her; they retreated and everyone left the scene unharmed.

Quickly, I re-enacted the scene. I had to believe the same would
happen for us.

Within a moment, I turned from a scarecrow into a wild animal.
Arms flung out, flapping like the wings of a huge eagle. A scream
leapt from me as I turned to face them. Screeching at the top of
my lungs, I charged towards the leader of the gang.
I felt empowered, larger than the bulls around us.
Strength and power saturated me like a mad scene from one of
Shakespeare's plays.

Intimidated they began to withdraw. Leaving us alone!
I witnessed this with both disbelief and relief.
Feeling my husband's hand in mine, he led me away to

safety, having spotted a small, wooden tower-like construction, surrounded by a fence up ahead of us. It was the only building in this deserted location.

We climbed up and into the tower, watching the bulls as they moved further away into the distance. We rested, giving thanks to God for sparing us.

When the bulls were merely specks, we lingered in gratitude. Descending to the ground where we walked as deer, on the alert for danger, quickly to the wire fence, crawling under and onward to safety.

A miracle!

An Outback Story

Caressing his blue check flannel shirt in both her hands, she gently with dreams of love, brought it to her face. With every inhalation, her nose, her eyes, her skin, were drenched in his smell. Her mind spun as she drew in breath after breath, stronger in an ecstatic knowing of her lover husband. He was gentle, yet giving passion of committed love to her. As she held his shirt allowing it to cradle her face; she knew she was so blessed.

He'd been gone only one day and she longed for his arms to wrap around her breathless chest. He'd gone mustering the cattle on horseback. She could smell the sweat and see his honest hard work. She held the shirt with both her hands, holding in each a shirt sleeve. She could see his sinews and smooth strong muscles. How she longed to have him near her. Yet she knew he'd be away for three more months. Taking the shirt, she sadly placed it to be washed with his other garments, soiled with dirt, grease and sweat. These would be sun dried, then folded ready and waiting for his return. Then after only ten days at home, the procedure would begin over again.

At home they would take many walks along the river, watch sun rises and sun sets together. Often he would throw in a line, make a camp fire and they would eat grilled fish straight from the wire rack with some damper and billy tea.

Lots of laughter happened as they would share tales of what the other had been doing while they were apart. He often would say to her: "One day I'll be coming home each night to you. These long separations will end." She lived in this hope.

He needed to do this for now to put food on their table and to make their small home as comfortable as could be. He was also saving to take her to the big city for a holiday, as a surprise for her. Whenever he could, he would buy her a little something special. Once he brought home a beautiful red dress and a small silver locket. More often he would pick her some wild flowers that he arranged with meticulous precision, demonstrating his love for her. The colours and perfumes almost matched her incredible joy of seeing him once more. When he was home she did her best to make special dishes of meat, vegetable and legumes for him.

He insisted on washing up, sweeping floors and hanging out the laundry for her. Then they would snuggle up together skins touching. Resting in each other's arms, strong arms that she grew to know and love. With his long fingers caressing her face and mouth. The days of parting were never easy for her. Yet she held on to that hope that one day he would stay with her forever and these lengthy separations would end.

It was a winter's morning. The air cuts the skin as broken glass, painful. He wore his long leather boots, woollen singlet and shirt and leather jacket. Under his long trousers, he wore a thin woollen trouser that she had knitted for him for the cold days ahead. They embraced; she lingered for another, then another kiss. He turned his back to her. She saw him riding away, with the heavy dew still on the ground.

The sun was beginning to shine. Leaving dappled leaves that clung to skinny branches. The landscape was sparsely dotted with scraggy greenish brown spindly shapes of small bushes which were scattered upon strips of brown, then darker brown merging into the pale blue horizon. As she stood alone in quiet confidence eeriness tingled over her whole body, as if she were the only mortal upon this earth.

She pleaded with God that he would soon return and never leave her again. The rising sun shed a soft pink glow all over the land. She stood a while taking in this beauty. For a while she forgot her loneliness and her desire to be with her husband. She saw the land washed with colours of pinks then reds and bright vermilions. She marvelled at this ever changing beauty. Hers to take, hers to drink in, hers to know what treasures she had each day, and they were free. She walked back to their little house, her feet noticing the dry cracked grounds. Opening her door she looked back at this never ending space of landscape. She thought

"no artist could capture this beauty, this stillness on a piece of canvas."
Before stepping inside she said: "and this is what he is riding into."

She began to busy herself with chores. Each day she would chop some wood for their fire, enough for when he would return, so he would not have to do this job. She sat and crocheted rugs and blankets, not only for themselves, but also for others who were in need, many struggling with children and new arrivals of babies. She made jams and marmalades to share with others. She made new shirts and trousers for her husband. A new coat and pants for herself. Then she made a number of little outfits for girls and boys.

She tended a not too large vegetable garden. Potatoes and pumpkins grew wild. She drew water from the river below and collected rainwater in tanks. Her work was never easy. Each evening she thanked God for another productive day and her ability to work. Each night she closed her eyes, giving thanks to the Lord for her husband and his safe return. She knew of the many dangers that he could encounter. It was work that required not only a fit body, but a quick wit of mind. It was hard work.

She slept soundly, awakening to early squawks of a group of birds, who sheltered in a nearby leafless tree. She drove into the small township every two to three weeks. Here she would buy some provisions of fruit, vegetables, flour and meat. They had two milking cows that she would milk early before sunrise and again before sunset. Later she would churn the milk, producing butter, cream and cheese. Chickens provided them with beautiful eggs. She also made marmalades from oranges and lemons. She was kept very busy, and as the time for his return approached, she would make an extra effort to make his arrival home very warm and special. He only longed to have her in his arms, kiss her and snuggle together, sometimes wildly chatting with each other, with news sharing events, and often they would say nothing at all. Just breathing in the love they had for each other. These thoughts crowded her mind as she thought of him being so far away from her.

"Only four more weeks" she said to herself with a spur of enthusiastic joy, imparting great energy to busy herself, to make ready the home for his impending entrance.

Suddenly a sickness, tiredness overtook her. She began to vomit. She drove herself to the town doctor, who upon examining her, told her that she was pregnant. A baby, his baby! Such joy flooded her that she did not care, that she would feel sick probably for the next few weeks. The thought of having a child growing within her womb, made her face shine with a glow that would never be erased or dimmed. When the shock of this news and the reality took hold of her, she was bursting with great joy and desire to tell her husband. She began counting the days, only one week to go until she would be in his arms again. She could hardly contain herself while thinking of how she would tell him the wonderful news. He would be a father to their darling child. Even though she was nauseous, she distracted herself turning the house into a home. After feeling sick she experienced great outbursts of energy.

The harsh flat landscape gave way to soft golden colours and the little shrubs seemed to glow as golden nuggets, growing up like flowers blossoming in spring. The leafless trees became wondrous sculptures with tiny leaves appearing, adorning the land with artistic wealth. Around her, and within her, was amazement at the wealth of love and beauty she had been gifted with. Praises and gratitude to the living God welled within every fibre of her being. At nights she lay contented thinking of the joy they would share together. Thoughts of him, the new life forming within her body, lulled her, like a familiar beautiful melody, in to a deep sleep. Days quickly passed. Soon he would be here.

One morning before the sun rose, she heard a clamouring at her door. She thought it was the wind so she ignored it. The noise, the knocking at her door grew louder. It was urgent. She sat upright and her feet touched the cold wooden floor. When she opened the door, she was surprised to see one of her husband's workmen standing there. She quickly invited him in, out of the cold. In the dim light she saw his pale drawn face. She hurried to make a fire, he helped her. Then offered him tea and some meat loaf she had made the previous day. "Please sit down, you must be so tired and where is my husband?" she softly pleaded. The man with head bowed low asked her to take a seat. "Some of the bulls went wild, broke loose." There was a deafening pause. She looked at him with such intensity that her veins felt as though they would pop out of her head. "Yes?" she interrupted his thoughts. "They bolted such as never

143

been seen before, rammed into his horse. He was thrown off. When we came to his aid he was dead. Bulls must have trampled him." She sat silently. The news did not register in her mind. Her heart pounded. "No" she screamed violently. Then she attacked the man thumping at his chest with her fists. "Please, please tell him to come home" she pleaded. He held her with gentleness feeling her grief. Then with tenderness she said to him "I've some wonderful news for him. He must come home so he'll be told." She went on with ramblings, inter-dispersed with sobbing and yelling. She could not, would not believe what she was hearing. She ran around the room in a frenzy of disbelief and agony. The horror of the news shattered her. She felt as though her heart and insides were being ripped out. She ran out of the door calling for her husband. She ran and screamed for a long time. He watched helplessly as she lay exhausted, broken on the damp, grassless grounds. He helped her back to the house, lifting her and carried her to her empty bed. He remained seated beside her until she awoke. He had already taken her husband's body to the town doctor and had informed the church minister. He helped the young woman into her car, and drove her into the town. Here she saw her husband. She ran to him, he looked as if asleep. She kissed his lips and stroked his cold face. She wanted to be left alone with him, snuggle up and lay cradled together. Just one final moment of reverence, where she could tell him about their baby and all the things she had done in the past three months. Respectfully they left her alone with him in a narrow single bed. She felt such peace and joy during this special time. She stroked his chest and his arms and wouldn't stop kissing his face. She even fell asleep. It seemed as though she slept for a few hours, it was maybe fifteen minutes? She was gently awakened by a nurse who told her that they had to make preparations for his burial. Still in shock she asked if she could help in washing him. Some friends arrived at the hospital. They were saddened by his death. He was a good man, and friend to many. They brought some spices and some oil. After he was bathed she dressed him in his favourite beige trousers and the lovely shirt she had recently made for him, along with his dark brown boots. She kissed his stone cold face. She thanked her friends then wept bitterly. Anger welled up within her, and she screamed to God momentarily for the injustice of her loss. Yet there was a joy for within her his child was growing. She nurtured this unborn one with great love. She decided to continue her life with joy. She made herself available to anyone who was in need financially, emotionally and spiritually. She was greatly used for good.

The birth came, and went. The child grew into a beautiful young boy. She continued to sew garments, and from the sales she was able to provide for her son a good education and also help those who found it difficult to make ends meet.

God blessed her greatly. She became well known for creating and sewing many household goods and her garments were of exceptional quality.

Her home often was filled with little children. Children, whose parents were in need of some respite or were very busy with work. She loved these times when mothers would gladly leave their children with her. They knew their children were safe with her, and were very happily occupied, and always well cared for. Her son was never lonely for a playmate. He had many. And she would teach the children about the love of God through Jesus Christ. She worked hard, prayed continuously to the Lord and was so grateful for what the Lord had given to her and her son.

Her son later left her to go to a university in a large city. He never forgot to write to her, and he would visit her on his holidays. He became a very fine doctor. Then he joined the Royal Flying Doctors to serve his community. His mother and friends were proud of this young man. He later married, and she never stopped being surrounded by happy, healthy children, including three of her own grand children.

She always remembered her husband, his love for her and others, and his care. At times she wished that he could be with her, to share in all her blessings. Sometimes sadness overtook her, but mostly there was joy in her life. She was grateful that she had many happy memories of loving times shared with her husband and for the gift from God, their son.

She died being loved by many, contented and at peace.

Blackbirds at the Beach

I've been watching, observing many times.
Black figures like egrets or penguins
slicing the air with precisioned direction, determination.
Riders on board, like comets, pursue their destination
being at one with syrupy waves
edged with white laceworks
smooth, fierce waves rise and fall.

Till to the white foamed sandy shore
they break and fall

With arms sprawled
there is a look of exhilaration upon their faces
as they retrieve their boards
then off to the paddle, back to the deep
to repeat this feat once again,
for hours, never stopping.
From daybreak to dusk.

I see their mates on the shore
leaning on fences, or watching from cliffs up high.
So absorbed with watching their sport
I thought to myself,
"What do they see in donning wetsuits,
heading for the beach and surf,
boards under their armpits
then, just standing on their surfboards

travelling to the shore, and back to the deep?"
What an idle, frivolous way to spend time, I thought.
What is the purpose of such sport?

Little did I know!
Till one afternoon, a well seasoned surfing man
asked me, while I was jumping up and down in waves,
having fun
"would you like to have a go?"
A little wary, I said "yes"

He said "Here, hop on board,
lay on your tummy and hold onto the front of the board."
Nervously I did as I was told.
I lay there and waited, hardly a breath,
cool water soothes my nerves.
Then, suddenly with a large wave
he pushed me out.

I sped upon those waters
as a star falling down from heaven.
I felt as though I was flying through the galaxies.
Space.
Passing stars and planets.
Exhilaration, beauty and freedom
enveloped all of me.

I felt like I was a little star
amongst the great vast universe.
The awe and wonder of God's creation.
So breathtaking, I screamed
in ecstatic delight, "I'm flying, so magnificent."
All trouble, cares, fears, disappeared.

I knew I was in God's hands,
so beautiful was this ride.
So memorable it is indelibly etched into my mind, forever.

I can never (and never want to), forget this moment.
So precious it is to me.

I wanted to ride those waves again and again and again
and I was lying down! Imagine how they feel – standing up on
top of their boards?
Now I know what they feel, what they do. What draws the surfer
to the sea!

I reluctantly gave back the board to the owner. With gratitude I
thanked him.
I could do this journey again and again and again.
These black birds flying through the air, across the seas,
have found a treasure and a jewel. Here they can play and feast
with God,
being at one with His creations.

Cold as Ice

Years ago a man and a woman met and married. She was a tall, rather unattractive woman, who was accustomed to living her life entirely to please herself. She was dull in appearance and without any substance of empathy for anyone else. She was quite hardened by the affluent life she had been brought up in. All her needs were met without any desire to share with anyone else. She learned to take and keep all for herself. She was friendless, yet in this she was comfortable. She had no goals to achieve. In fact one would call her boring within and without. No appreciation over anything of beauty in nature or character. She lived an empty life, never seeing or hearing the beauty of birds or their songs. She held a typists job for a firm that sent out letters for various companies. She did not stay long as she found it tedious to communicate with others and she was not reliant on any income. All she thought about was how she could please herself. She absorbed herself in empty romantic novels, written as though for her, shallow, without much substance. Tinsel, empty, arousing flesh desires, superficial. No realities of life. She had a straight up and down figure, no curves. She looked highly unfeminine. Yet she had a confidence within herself. She continuously delighted to criticize wherever, whenever and whomever she pleased. So she lived, with a torte, bitter face appearance. Most people kept away from her. She was known as a gossiping busybody. Then she met a young man, who too was shallow in his outlook on life. He was boring and without any excitement in his life. He worked in a little office doing odd jobs. Somewhat shabby in appearance, they were instantly attracted to each other, decided to marry, and put down a deposit on a small, very ordinary house, in a very ordinary location. Here they lived for many years. They took no interest in their surroundings or in people.

As the years went by and their financial position blossomed, they still did the same things. Daily they went to the local shops, came home, watched television. They showed no interest in making a nice garden or to beautify their home of many years. They lived a drab existence, with no children, with barely a visitor. They lived to all appearances, utterly selfish lives. As they grew older, they were very comfortable; they rarely became ill and never interacted with their community. How can people live like this?

After observing a neighbour who often had visitors, families with little children, they noticed that there was always a lot of laughter and joyful noises coming from that home.

They were envious, thought they should do the same. So they approached an organisation that helped children who are in need of support and kindness.

A social worker visited this couple. They passed essential criteria, having a home that was safely structured with a fenced yard, they were in a very good financial position and they had plenty of room and time to spend with a child. The lady entered the house with a little boy. She felt there was coldness within. The couple sat rigid, and forced a smile that betrayed crooked teeth.

No sign of emotion or joy. The child was a bright boy of seven years who had recently been orphaned. His parents died in a car accident. The child was devastated. He needed much emotional support and special care. He rarely smiled these days; he was dazed and became withdrawn. On the few occasions that he smiled, his face would glow like a light bulb switched on to high beam, displaying a beautiful smile. The boy was astute and intelligent. He sat quietly not saying a word, feeling uncomfortable with the couple in this room. They didn't even offer a cup of tea to the lady, or a drink with a biscuit to the child. The lady asked some questions of the couple. There were moments of great awkwardness and even silence. After some time, the couple said that they would think about taking the boy over a short period of time, or until a more permanent arrangement could be made.

After saying goodbye, the lady thanked them for their time. She took the little boys hand and as the door closed behind them she felt relieved and said to herself: "No, I could not leave the boy with them, he would be very unhappy, and isolated." She was so relieved when the old woman rang two days later, saying that they decided not to take in the little boy.

The lady had grown very fond of the child, and as they got to know each other, she decided to keep the boy herself. She approached the organisation, and also her husband and her two children, who were only one and two years older than this child. All were in agreement. She then asked the child. His smile was so big that it stayed on his face a long while. Her children eagerly got to making his bed and sharing all their toys with him. They were so happy having him at their picnic outings and going to the supermarket with them. They even told everyone that he was their new brother. School and sports were organised. The boy grew up to become a talented surgeon. He made his services available for poorer communities, bearing many costs himself.

The old couple had turned down the opportunity to show some kindness and help a child. They remained being selfish. Their bitterness froze upon their faces, and their blood continued to run cold as ice through their veins.

The Marriage

Anne and Jim were married on a sunny, early afternoon in a church where Anne attended with her parents as a child.

Spacious with ornamental frescos etched in gilded gold decorated some of the walls. Sunlight poured colours upon the floor and pews, from stained glass windows, some of which depicted stories of Christ, His life and His disciples. Like a bowl of coloured jellies, these were mixed by the sunlight – greens, golds, vermilions and reds. She looked so beautiful in her carefully chosen, expertly made white gown. Lace trimmings and the train had everyone sitting in awe of this bride. Hair pulled up showed off her swan-like neck and held in place by a brilliant shining tiara. Her dainty arms and hands covered by lace hung loosely by her side. Music played as the groom stood awaiting his bride. Though nervous in awaiting her, he projected pride and happiness in her appearance. His heart beat had to be contained by his mind. He loved her dearly. Said she was the girl that he wanted to be with for the rest of his life.

His mother was a little apprehensive when her son announced to her that he would marry the girl that he wanted as his wife. He was young, so was she. His mother thought and said "perhaps you should wait a while, as you've only known each other for six months, then you get engaged." Wedding plans were made after another six months. His mother was so happy for his joy and his unrelenting eagerness to marry this girl. She did all she could to embrace her into her life, and she did all that she could to contribute to the marriage. Though short in stature, looking like a porcelain doll, she came across as quite intelligent and presented herself as a future, loving wife, who would care for and respect her son. Mother accepted with humility that her son and his bride would have a happy, healthy, well adjusted marriage. Though she did not meet her acquaintance too often, she saw only good in the girl and her external prettiness mesmerised the mother. She thought they were a very well suited couple and was confident that their marriage would endure a lifetime of prosperity and blessing.

And it did!

Author Biography

Katarina is of Russian parentage. She was born in Germany but now resides in Sydney, Australia, after migrating at the age of 6.

Upon landing in Australia, her family were placed in a camp in Cowra, along with other migrants of many different nationalities. During her time there, Katarina, who already spoke Russian, became fluent at German, Polish, Latvian and, of course English.

Katarina's family were forced to live in a tin shed that was later sold for use as a chook pen. She became accustomed to living in a red-back spider infested environment and often encountered snakes on the way to her beloved school.

Her saving grace was education. Katarina was encouraged and well-liked by her teachers.

After this, her family moved to Sydney, where she was subjected to racist bullying and a difficult environment. She was spurred on by her academic achievements, she found solace through her drawing and writing and was encouraged by pivotal figures in her life.

More than anything else, her faith in God caused her to turn her life around, and ultimately led to the creation of this book.

Printed in the United States
by Baker & Taylor Publisher Services